ERRATA

p.7 Table:	Resale pri........

p.8 Under Table: .... at ... end of this year that the replacement should be made.

p.17 Example 4:   Each project has three possible outcomes.

Project 1.   E.P.V. = -3 x 0.3 + 2 x 0.2
                              + 4 x 0.5
              E.P.V. = + 1.5

Project 2.   E.P.V. = -1 x 0.10 + 1 x 0.4
                              + 2 x 0.5
              E.P.V. = + 1.3

Project 3.   E.P.V. = 0.5 x 0.6 + 1.5 x 0.3
                              + 3 x 0.1
              E.P.V. = +1.05

p.19   .... Project 3, Figure 2.9 at £1.05 millions.

p.46-48 Figures 3.3-3.5: $15,004,000 to read $14,905,000

p.48 Top line: $14,269,675 to read $14,205,000

p.50 Second paragraph: Medium yield 0.4.

p.52 Top line: $7,725,000 to read $7,775,000
                  $6,387,000 to read $7,087,000
                  Medium yield 0.4.

p.59   Buy 300 crates will lose £375
        Buy 400 crates will lose £1,312.5
        Loss of £2312.5 if buy 500 crates

p.62   E.M.V. 267,600 to read 267,200
        E.M.V. = (0.86 x 25,000 x 8) + (0.14 x 40,000
                      x 8)

p.63   E.M.V. = 0.7 (45,000 x 2 + 267,200) + 0.3
                      (40,000 x 10) - 130,000 = 240,040.

p.64 Second line: Large - High - Low + (8 x 10,000)

p.75   Activity L preceded by H and J and K

p.88 Alternative
     solution: Reduce F and N by 1 day @ £190
                  then F and L by 1 day @ £200
                  then B   by 1 day @ £250
                  Total cost 40 days   @ £17,190

p.114 Paragraph 3: .... at one port.

p.132 Example 1: Two hours through B.

p.139 Equation 14: $+ \dfrac{S5_B}{3}$

p.139 Last paragraph: £10 to read £20

p.156 3rd Matrix: interchange profit values 80 and 100

p.162 First Equation: £2,000x + £5,000y __ 120,000
restrictions: x __ 20
y __ 10
x + y __ 50

p.169 Constraints: = 26, = 242, = 2,700, = 250 respectively

p.172 Junction N.C: 0.11 to read 0.66
bottom S_2 column: -18 to read 4.20
bottom calcul-
ation: $\dfrac{7.2}{0.66} = 10.9$

p.173 Junction I.N: -0.48
Junction S_4N: -0.18
MS 3: 223 to read -89
bottom S_2: -17.3 to read 4.9
C: 3.8
Total profit: approximately £3,088

p.176 Under Table: January figure 1974 + January figure 1975

DA 3

QUANTITATIVE AIDS FOR MANAGEMENT DECISION MAKING

Quantitative Aids for Management Decision Making

With Applications

C. F. PALMER

Development Administration Group,
Institute of Local Government Studies,
University of Birmingham

SAXON HOUSE

© C. F. Palmer 1979

 British Library Cataloguing in Publication Data

Palmer, C F
  Quantitative aids for management decision
  making.
  1. Decision-making - Mathematical models
  I. Title
  658.4'03   HD30.23

  ISBN 0-566-00248-1

Published by
Teakfield Limited,
Westmead, Farnborough, Hants., England

ISBN   0 566 00284 1

Printed in Great Britain by David Green (Printers) Ltd, Kettering, Northamptonshire

Contents

Preface

The book should be suitable for those with only a limited background in mathematics and statistics and only a knowledge of elementary algebra and basic matrix algebra is required. In certain cases a knowledge of statistics including some probability and theory of distributions is assumed, but it is anticipated that the student should have little difficulty in following the texts of each chapter.

The book only attempts to introduce the methods, techniques or 'aids to decision-making' and should the reader wish to pursue the subject further it is hoped that the bibliography covering each chapter will assist in this direction.

Use is made of examples to develop any method or technique that is introduced in the texts. This system has proved very effective when teaching the methods to students with a limited quantitative background. Generally at the end of each text there are examination type questions complete with solutions to enable the reader to test his knowledge of the methods introduced.

What the writer considers is perhaps the most important part of the book and one of its main objectives, is the introduction of a section for each chapter covering the application of methods discussed, to problems found in industry. This section will enable the reader to study the problem and offer his own solution and conclusions. Solutions are given to the applications, but a discussion section enables a variation to the original problem to be introduced and thus the reader can again test his ability in solving a realistic problem.

The projects or applications could be used by tutors to supplement their teaching of the theory where time permits. It could be argued that they are of greater value than the examination type question which has usually to be completed in forty-five to sixty minutes, compared with the time necessary to solve these types of problems in the 'real' world.

In many cases a unique solution is not possible and a 'good' solution is all that we can obtain within the constraints surrounding the problem. Except perhaps in the chapter on Linear Programming where the solutions are unique, hopefully the solutions presented are 'good', but the reader is invited to improve on these where possible.

I would like to thank the Institute of Local Government Studies, without whose support this book would not have been possible, Jill Fussell for typing the script and Tim Grogan for the art work.

1 Decision making

Decisions taken by management will always have to be based on judgement. But decisions have to be made for a future which will continue to be unpredictable and these decisions will always entail risks. Anything that can make the task easier, or 'aids to decision making', would be welcomed by management. Some of these will be discussed in the Chapters to follow.

By the use of a procedure which involves four basic steps, an improvement in decision making can be made. These four basic steps are:-

1. Make a careful definition of the problem.
2. Define the objectives.
3. Endeavour to develop alternative solutions.
4. Applying the decision once made.

1. DEFINITION OF THE PROBLEM

This is probably the most important step, as too many businessmen tend to spend an excessive amount of time searching for the answer rather than spend time finding out what the problem really is. We could commence with the question, 'Is there a problem?' Assuming there is a problem to be solved and by making a definition of what the problem really is, we can often reduce what appears to be a large messy problem with many variables and factors, to one where the issues, although not soluble by the use of techniques alone, are focused on fewer variables and factors.

At this stage the question of, 'What risks can we afford to take?' becomes the basic one. Risks of not meeting a specific target date, loss of customers because of particular marketing decisions and the possibility of idle men and plant through production scheduling decisions and whether money could be better invested elsewhere are but a few that can arise.

Every decision is an attempt to balance gains, costs and risks. Very often we pick the solution which has the lowest costs even though it promises the lowest gains and greatest risk. A decision should be looked upon as an opportunity rather than a problem.

An attempt to quantify wherever possible should be made, but it is appreciated that all decisions cannot be based on figures alone and not all risks can be listed.

2 DEFINE THE OBJECTIVE

In forecasting we endeavour to project into the future based only on facts we have from the past. The importance is to collect the 'relevant' facts and having obtained these the actual decision is based on some future objective.

We need to define our objective in relation to the problem being studied whether it be profit, cost etc. In defining the objective we can avoid the unnecessary collection and presentation of irrelevant data. At the same time we will probably realise that not all the facts are available and areas requiring the powers of estimation are required.

3. ALTERNATIVE SOLUTIONS

In all problems there are constraints or restrictions whether it be men, material or money, but we must be sure that we consider within these restrictions the full range of solutions that are possible. The solutions must meet our objective and within the risk we have decided that we can afford.

What is important, is that time should be available for management to receive the fullest information on the alternatives that exist and time to choose between these alternatives.

Considering all the alternatives is also the only way we have to make sure that we do not overlook opportunities.

4. APPLYING THE DECISION

Knowing the range of alternatives that exist, the resources available to meet the alternatives, the objectives set and risks involved, we need to be able to compare courses of action against these objectives and risks. The best course of action is rarely obvious and without some risk, although some may appear more desirable than others. It is often by using some of the techniques to be discussed in later Chapters that we can narrow down the judgement necessary in decision making and also why such decisions have been made.

We need the means to measure the effectiveness of the decision made, against performance objectives over intervals of time. Although we cannot expect perfect correlation between objective and performance, careful monitoring can assist in future decision making by highlighting errors between 'forecast' and 'actual' and enable this difference to be taken into consideration in any future decisions.

Last, but by no means least, we should realise that others carry out the actions of the decision and therefore they should understand why certain decisions were made.

We have constantly referred to risk and uncertainty and further discussion on these would be appropriate.

Decisions are made under conditions of:-

1. Certainty

   If each action is known to lead to some specific outcome.

2. Risk

   If each action leads to one of a number of possible specific outcomes, with each of the outcomes occurring with a known probability.

3. Uncertainty

   If each action leads to one of a number of possible specific outcomes, but in this case the probabilities of these outcomes are not known.

In considering 1, decision making under certainty, given a set of possible actions, we choose one or more of these actions which maximises or minimises some set criteria. The difficulties with this are two fold -

(a) The number of possible actions can be very great and it is not always possible to state them. The use of Linear Programming discussed in a later Chapter can assist in this area.

(b) The choice of some criteria. In many examples the choice of profit or loss is appropriate. In others no suitable criteria can be immediately recognisable or possible.

In 2, the area of risk where the probabilities of each occurring outcome is known we can use the following example, to assist in our decision.

EXAMPLE 1

A village in an overseas country has to decide which crop to plant. Their choice is limited to 'surface' or 'root' crops, depending upon the rainfall which can be put into three categories, heavy, medium or light. Data is available to them from the local ministry on the probability of rainfall being in these categories for the coming season. These probabilities are:

Heavy rainfall	=	.30
Medium rainfall	=	.40
Light rainfall	=	.30
Total		1.00

The total probabilities will equal one because these are the only possible outcomes.

We form what is known as a 'pay-off matrix'

		X_1	X_2	X_3
		Heavy Rainfall	Medium Rainfall	Light Rainfall
		0.30	0.40	0.30
	Crops			
Y_1	Surface	$40,000	$30,000	$20,000
Y_2	Root	$70,000	$20,000	---

The possible monetary returns to be received by the village is shown in the appropriate column for each crop under specific rainfall.

The problem is which crop should the village sow? We use the concept of 'expected value' which is the probability of occurrence multiplied by the value (profit or loss). The summation of these calculations gives us the 'total expected value' (T.E.V.) and we choose the 'maximum expected value' in the case of profit. Considering surface crops we have the total expected value of:-

$$\text{T.E.V.} = (40,000 \times 0.3) + (30,000 \times 0.4) + (20,000 \times 0.3)$$

$$\text{T.E.V.} = (12,000) + (12,000) + (6,000)$$

$$\text{T.E.V.} = \$30,000$$

In considering root crops we have the total expected value of:-

$$\text{T.E.V.} = (70,000 \times 0.3) + (20,000 \times 0.4) + (0)$$

$$\text{T.E.V.} = (21,000) + (8,000)$$

$$\text{T.E.V.} = \$29,000$$

The decision maker would by this method choose to plant surface crops where the maximum expected value was $30,000.

In 3, under conditions of uncertainty, the problems become more complicated. Here the probabilities of the outcomes are not known. We can take a second example to see the possibilities.

EXAMPLE 2

A large organisation is considering the investment of money in one of three possible areas. The economic situation of the country has

4

has varied a great deal over recent years and three stages of interest
rates will affect their decision, High, Medium or Low. The expected
returns are placed against the area of investment and interest rate
category in the form of 'pay-off matrix' as in the previous example.

	I_1	II_2	II_3
	High Interest Rate	Medium Interest Rate	Low Interest Rate
Area 1 Manufacturing	$180,000	$40,000	$-30,000
Area 2 Catering	$ 80,000	$70,000	---
Area 3 Leisure	$ 15,000	$15,000	$ 15,000

In this example we have no knowledge of probabilities on which we can
base any decisions therefore the maximum expected value method used
in Example 1 is not applicable here. An alternative criteria is
necessary, two of these will now be considered.

(i) The 'maximin method'

Here it is suggested that the decision maker should always be
completely pessimistic. If we regard the state of the market as
a 'state of nature' then the decision maker should act as though
nature would be completely malevolent once he had chosen his
strategy and as if she would choose a state which would always
minimise his pay-off. Let us assume that area 1 had been chosen
for investment then the worst that could happen is a loss of
$30,000. Should area 2 be chosen then returns would be 0 profit
with low interest rate as previous and finally should we choose
area 3 then the worst would again be under a low interest rate
and $15,000 profit. Forming a pay-off matrix:

Minimum Pay-Off

Area 1	- $30,000
Area 2	---
Area 3	$15,000

The largest of these minimum pay-offs, which is the maximum of
the minimum, thus the same 'maximin method' would be $15,000 and
we should therefore choose to invest in area 3.

(ii) The 'maximax method'·

Here we have the reverse situation that of being completely
optimistic. The idea is, that why should we always consider
that the worst is going to happen? If we take this idea and

5

use the previous example we obtain a pay-off matrix thus:

Best of Maximum Pay-Off

Area 1	$180,000
Area 2	$ 80,000
Area 3	$ 15,000

Thus if the decision maker considers that high interest rates
will occur, then an investment in area 1 will be the decision
made. This is therefore the 'maximax'.

A refinement on the method is where the decision-maker can take into
account both the largest and smallest pay-off for each strategy. He
could weight their importance to his decision in accordance with his
own feeling of optimism. For instance if the decision-maker feels
that the weight towards optimism is 7/10 then he would arrange the
maximum and minimum pay-offs as follows:-

	Maximum Pay-Off	Minimum Pay-Off
Area 1	180	-30
Area 2	80	0
Area 3	15	15

Expected Pay-Off

Area 1	$(180 \times 7/10) + (-30 \times 3/10)$	= 117
Area 2	$(80 \times 7/10) + (0 \times 3/10)$	= 56
Area 3	$(15 \times 7/10) + (15 \times 3/10)$	= 15

The decision would be to invest in area 1 which is the maximum
expected pay-off.

Much more complex decision questions can be portrayed in pay-off
table form. However, particularly for complex investment decisions,
a different representation of the information can be made in the form
of the 'decision tree', which will be discussed in Chapter Three.

2 Replacement

In this section four areas will be discussed:

1. Equipment that gradually deteriorates over a period of time and the correct time for replacement.

2. Items that fail suddenly with consideration to alternative methods of replacement.

3. Discounted Cash Flow (D.C.F.) and other methods of assessing an investment.

4. The concept of risk in making investments.

1. REPLACEMENT OF EQUIPMENT THAT DETERIORATES WITH TIME

Having purchased equipment the cost may be considered as an average cost/unit time which could be spread over its total life. An assumption can be made, that, as the life of the equipment increases, the cost of maintenance will increase and that the overall efficiency will decrease. The basic problem is to balance the burden of capital cost with the increased running cost.

Whilst the theory is comparatively simple, the problem of obtaining correct maintenance figures particularly past data which is easily accessible, is considerable. Experience combined with historical data is necessary to project maintenance costs which will vary considerably from machine to machine, depending upon the usage by both operator and type of work undertaken.

EXAMPLE 1

A machine was purchased for the sum of £7,000. It has been possible to obtain data of maintenance costs for the same type of machine and present resale prices. Based on this information, when would be the correct time, based on costs, to replace?

Year	1	2	3	4	5
Running costs	1,200	1,400	1,600	2,000	2,500
Resale price	3,200	1,700	950	575	400

Year	6	7	8	9	10
Running costs	3,000	3,600	4,200	4,600	5,200
Resale price	400	400	400	200	200

Over the ten year period we can calculate the cumulative total running costs which is shown in column (2), Table 2.1. In column (3) we show the cumulative capital costs which are the purchase cost - resale price. By obtaining the product of these two, the total costs are entered in column (4). The average costs per year are obtained by dividing column (4) by the year under consideration from column (1).

Table 2.1.

Costs of owning and operating a machine

Replace at end of year	Total Running Costs (£)	Total Capital Cost (£)	Total Cost (£)	Average Cost per year
(1)	(2)	(3)	(4) (2)+(3)	(5)
1	1,200	3,800	5,000	5,000
2	2,600	5,300	7,900	3,950
3	4,200	6,050	10,250	3,416
4	6,200	6,425	12,625	3,156
5	8,700	6,600	15,300	3,060
6	11,700	6,600	18,300	3,050
7	15,300	6,600	21,900	3,128
8	19,500	6,600	26,100	3,262
9	24,100	6,800	30,900	3,433
10	29,300	6,800	36,100	3,610

The average costs are at a minimum in year 6 at £3,050 and it is at this time the replacement should be made.

2. REPLACEMENT OF ITEMS WITH SUDDEN FAILURE

In this category we place items that are assumed to be working normally until they reach a point where they suddenly cease to function correctly. The parts that have failed are then replaced by new identical parts. The mathematics of this category can be complex, but many basic principles are worth consideration.

EXAMPLE 2

A computer has 500 important valves which have to be replaced when a failure occurs. The problem concerns when it would be more economical to replace, either individually on failure or to replace all valves at regular intervals and only then replace individuals as they fail between these intervals. Data has been stored on the failure rates of these types of valves which is shown in the following table.

Week	1	2	3	4	5
Per cent failing by the end of week	5	15	40	70	100

The cost of replacing an individual valve is estimated to be £1.50. and the cost of replacing all 500 is £150. What would be the best policy to adopt?

Reviewing the information we have available, we know that no valve will last after five weeks and therefore any valve working after the fourth week will fail during the fifth week. From the probabilities given we can obtain the failure rates of valves for each of the five weeks, e.g. Week 1 the probability of failure is 5% or 0.05, Week 2 = 15-5 = 10% or 0.10 and so on to obtain the table following:

Week	Probability that a new valve fitted at time zero fails during week (X)
(X)	(P_x)
1	0.05
2	0.10
3	0.25
4	0.30
5	0.30
	____
	1.00

By making two assumptions we can arrive at the number of replacements due to fail in successive weeks, under a policy of no group replacement. We assume: (a) that valves that fail during a week are replaced just before the end of that week; (b) that the actual percentage of failures during a week for a sub-population of valves with the same age is the same as the expected percentage of failures during the week for that sub-population.

Let n_0 equal the number of original new valves and n_1 equal the number of replacements made at the end of the first week, n_2 at the end of the second and so on. Under the assumptions made we can calculate the number of failures each week.

To calculate n_1 we have 500 valves with probability of 0.05 failure in this first week which gives 500 x 0.05 = 25 failures. In the second week, n_2, of the 25 replaced at the end of the first week there will be a probability of 0.05 they will fail in the second week (their first) and those that did not fail in the first week have a probability of 0.10 of failing in the second. Thus for n_2 we have $n_0 p_2 + n_1 p_1$ = 500 x 0.10 + 25 x 0.05 = 50 + 1.25, say 52 valves. The same logic follows for the weeks following.

9

$$n_0 = n_0 \qquad\qquad = 500$$

$$n_1 = n_0 p_1 \quad = \quad 500 \times 0.05 \qquad\qquad = 25$$

$$n_2 = n_0 p_2 + n_1 p_1 \quad = \quad 500 \times 0.10 + 25 \times 0.05 \quad = \quad 50 + 1.25 \quad = 52$$

$$n_3 = n_0 p_3 + n_1 p_2 + n_2 p_1 \quad = \quad 125 + 2.5 + 2.6 \qquad = 131$$

$$n_4 = n_0 p_4 + n_1 p_3 + n_2 p_2 + n_3 p_1 \qquad\qquad = 168$$

$$n_5 = n_0 p_5 + n_1 p_4 + n_2 p_3 + n_3 p_2 + n_4 p_1 \qquad = 192$$

$$n_6 = \qquad n_1 p_5 + n_2 p_4 + n_3 p_3 + n_4 p_2 + n_5 p_1 \qquad = 83$$

$$n_7 = \qquad\qquad n_2 p_5 + n_3 p_4 + n_4 p_3 + n_5 p_2 + n_6 p_1 \qquad = 121$$

If we observe the table, the failures increase until week 5 and then
decrease and if the calculations were carried farther the failures
again increase and continue to oscillate until ultimately the
failures rates settle down to what is known as a 'steady state' in
which the proportion of valves failing each week is the reciprocal of
their average life. The average life is calculated for the figures
presented.

$$(1 \times 0.05) \quad + \quad (2 \times 0.10) \quad + \quad (3 \times 0.25) + (4 \times 0.30) + (5 \times 0.30)$$

$$= \quad 0.05 \quad + \quad 0.20 \quad + \quad 0.75 \quad + \quad 1.20 \quad + \quad 1.5$$

$$= \quad 3.70$$

Therefore in the steady state the number of failures each week will be

$$\frac{500}{3.70} \quad = \quad 135$$

If the policy of replacing is by failure then the costs would be
135 x £1.50.   = £202.50. per week.

An alternative policy would be to consider replacing failures during
week 1 and group replace at the end of the same week at a cost of
£150 + 25 x £1.50.   = £187.50. per week.

Replacing all valves at the end of two weeks and during weeks 1 and
2 involve costs of £150 + 25 x £1.50 + 52 x £1.50 = £265.50. This
gives an average of £132.75. per week.

If all valves were replaced at the end of three weeks and during
weeks 1, 2 and 3 the cost would be £150 + £37.50 + £78 + 131 x £1.50.
= £462, giving an average of £154 per week.

The cheapest policy of the four considered would be to replace after
two weeks at an average of £132.75. per week.

3. DISCOUNTED CASH FLOW (D.C.F.) AND OTHER METHODS OF ASSESSING AN INVESTMENT

Before discussing the principles of D.C.F. it is worth reviewing two accountancy methods used for appraising investment.

    1. The return expected over 'x' number of years.

    2. The date at which a project 'breaks even'.

1. The return expected over 'x' number of years

    This method is usually adopted for projects over a five to ten year period, but in certain major developments the period is extended.

    The problem with this method is that it does not take into consideration any savings beyond the specified period and is not able to assess the difference between different distributions of returns, each having the same total, over the period. Examples of this problem are illustrated below.

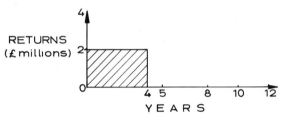

Figure 2.1. Cash returns, years 0-4

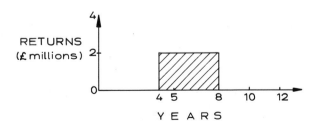

Figure 2.2. Cash returns, years 4-8.

11

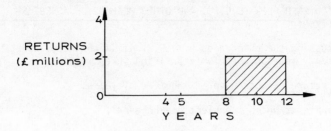

RETURNS
(£ millions)

YEARS

Figure 2.3. Cash returns, years 8-12.

The three projects being appraised have the same return over a
four year period but in Figure 2.1. it is in the first four years
of the twelve year period, in Figure 2.2. the middle four and
Figure 2.3. shows the returns during the last four years of the
period. The method has no means of differentiating between the
three.

2. The date at which a project 'breaks even'

In an attempt to improve on the previous method, the date at which
a project 'breaks even' was considered as an appraisal method.
If we take the previous three examples and find that the break
even point in Figure 2.1. is three years, in Figure 2.2. is seven
years, and finally in Figure 2.3. eleven years, then the project
of Figure 2.1. would stand out above the other two, as the break
even point is reached earlier.

Unfortunately the method is unable to say how much one investment
is better than another over their whole lives, which is surely
what is required.

If we consider again three projects:

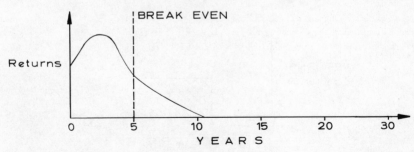

Figure 2.4. Distribution of cash returns.

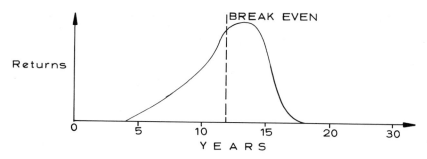

Figure 2.5. Distribution of cash returns.

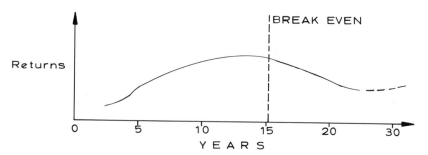

Figure 2.6. Distribution of cash returns.

Using the methods already discussed we would rank the project shown in Figure 2.4. as being superior to the other two, with Figure 2.5. as second choice, finally Figure 2.6. In fact in Figure 2.6. the return will be substantial beyond the twenty year mark and possibly this would be management's choice above the other two. However, neither method is adequate to show in quantitative terms the superiority of one project over another and they do not include the concept of time into the analysis of return.

Discounted cash flow (D.C.F.) does take into account the importance of time and although not ideal it is an improvement on the previous methods.

Since money has a time value, future expenditures and opportunity costs will have different present or current values to us. First we must explain the meaning of time value and money.

The basis of D.C.F. is that one pound today is worth more than one pound in a year's time. For example, if a pound was borrowed from the bank at 10 per cent interest per annum and if it were to be invested with a sum returned at the end of the year, this amount would have to be greater than £1 x (1.10) to make the initial borrowing worthwhile.

We will use the following terms to develop the principle further:

Let P = Principal sum to be invested
R = Rate of interest or expected rate of return
n = number of years
S = future total sum

Using the above we know that if a principal sum P is invested at an interest rate R, it will yield a future total sum S in n years hence, that is if all of the earnings are retained and compounded. Therefore P in the present is entirely equivalent to S in the future by value of the compound amount factor:

$$S = P (1 + R)^n$$

where $(1 + R)^n$ is equal to the compound amount factor for interest rate R and n years.

We can similarly solve for P to determine the present worth of a sum to be paid in n years hence:

$$P = \frac{S}{(1 + R)^n} = S \times PVS$$

where PVS = the present value of a single payment S to be made n years hence, with interest R.

To apply figures to the equations, assume a payment of £5,000 in ten years. We assume that we would accept a smaller but equivalent sum now. For ease of calculation a 10 per cent interest was considered suitable and the equivalent amount would be P.

$$P = S \times PVS$$

$$\text{and } PVS = \frac{1}{(1 + R)^n}$$

$$\text{therefore } PVS = \frac{1}{(1 + 0.10)^n} = 0.3855$$

$$\text{and } P = 5,000 \times 0.3855 = £1,927$$

If all future values were adjusted to the present as a common base time, we could compare the totals to see which of the alternative investments was the most attractive.

EXAMPLE 3

A company wishes to invest in a new machine costing £20,000. Two
different models are available each being suitable for the particular
task and, within a few pounds, both can be obtained for the sum
mentioned. Figures have been obtained from the suppliers of
estimated operating costs over a ten year period and resale values
for the same length of time. Using an interest rate of 10 per cent,
the company wish D.C.F. to be applied to the problem and a decision
made regarding which model should be purchased.

	Model 1			Model 2	
Year	Operating Cost	Capital Cost	Year	Operating Cost	Capital Cost
	(£)	(£)		(£)	(£)
1	500	1,000	1	700	2,000
2	700	3,000	2	800	3,500
3	900	5,000	3	900	4,500
4	1,100	7,000	4	1,000	6,000
5	1,400	10,000	5	1,100	8,000
6	1,700	11,000	6	1,200	9,000
7	1,900	12,000	7	1,900	10,000
8	2,000	14,000	8	2,500	12,000
9	2,400	16,000	9	2,600	14,000
10	2,600	18,000	10	3,000	17,000

In the following tables 2.2 and 2.3. the operating costs and capital
costs are obtained from the data given and entered in columns (2) and
(3). The combined costs consist of column (2) + column (3) and
entered in column (4). The present worth factor (P.W.) is obtained
from the table shown on page 197, for the year indicated to form
column (5). Finally column (6) is the P.W. factor multiplied by the
combined operating and capital costs.

From these tables, Model 1 would be the most attractive proposition.

When calculating for present worth the effect of the value R is
apparent. This figure has to be agreed and a certain amount of
controversy has been aroused over the value. One could suggest that
it be the current bank rate because money can be borrowed at this
rate. However, if all one's projects were evaluated by this means
one could never have a profitable organisation and there would be
no point in borrowing from the bank.

It seems both sensible and reasonable that to use a value of R
which is compatible with the average earning power of existing
investment 'within the organisation' and of future investments to be
undertaken by the organisation. In this way any money not used on
one project can be distributed over other projects and earn approximately the same rate of return.

15

Table 2.2.

Present value, operating and capital costs for Model 1

Year	Operating Cost	Capital Cost	Combined Operating and Capital Cost	P.W. Factor	P.W. of Combined Costs
(1)	(2)	(3)	(4)	(5)	(6)
1	500	1,000	1,500	0.909	1,363
2	700	3,000	3,700	0.826	3,056
3	900	5,000	5,900	0.751	4,430
4	1,100	7,000	8,100	0.683	5,532
5	1,400	10,000	11,400	0.621	7,079
6	1,700	11,000	12,700	0.565	7,175
7	1,900	12,000	13,900	0.513	7,130
8	2,000	14,000	16,000	0.467	7,472
9	2,400	16,000	18,400	0.424	7,801
10	2,600	18,000	20,600	0.386	7,951

Total £58,989

Table 2.3.

Present value, operating and capital costs for Model 2

Year	Operating Cost	Capital Cost	Combined Operating and Capital Cost	P.W. Factor	P.W. of Combined Costs
(1)	(2)	(3)	(4)	(5)	(6)
1	700	2,000	2,700	0.909	2,454
2	800	3,500	4,300	0.826	3,551
3	900	4,500	5,400	0.751	4,055
4	1,000	6,000	7,000	0.683	4,781
5	1,100	8,000	9,100	0.621	5,651
6	1,200	9,000	10,200	0.565	5,763
7	1,900	10,000	11,900	0.513	6,104
8	2,500	12,000	14,500	0.467	6,771
9	2,600	14,000	16,600	0.424	7,038
10	3,000	17,000	20,000	0.386	7,720

Total £53,888

4. THE CONCEPT OF RISK IN MAKING INVESTMENTS

In all of the three methods discussed, whether it be costs or returns on investment the figures quoted have been definite values. There has been no element of doubt that in a particular year these figures will occur. Usually it is not possible to predict an exact cost or return from a project after a few years with a great deal of certainty. Obviously any financial return that is dependent upon such variables as market conditions is open to unpredictable fluctuations over, say, a ten year period.

In these situations a further factor could be considered, that of 'probability'. It is suggested that an investment should have its returns calculated with probabilities associated. To make a realistic investment appraisal the following approach may take us a step forward from D.C.F. and is worth consideration.

EXAMPLE 4

Three projects are due for appraisal. The principle of D.C.F. has been applied to arrive at the present worth or present value for comparison and the range of possible outcomes regarding costs (outflow) and return (inflow) are shown in Figures 2.7., 2.8. and 2.9. Each project has four possible outcomes shown by the vertical bars. The range of present values in £(millions) is the horizontal axis and the probability of occurrence of these outcomes is the vertical axis.

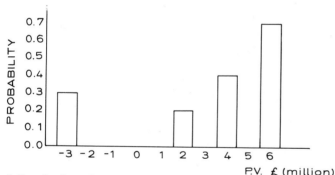

Figure 2.7. Project 1.

To evaluate the expect net present value of the projects, we use the concept that the expected value or mathematical expectation is the weighted average of the possible results anticipated from a particular course of action, where the weights are the probabilities.

Project 1 Expected Present Value (E.P.V.)

E.P.V. = -3 x 0.3 + 2 x 0.2 + 4 x 0.4 + 6 x 0.6
E.P.V. = -0.9 + 0.4 + 1.6 + 3.6
E.P.V. = +4.7

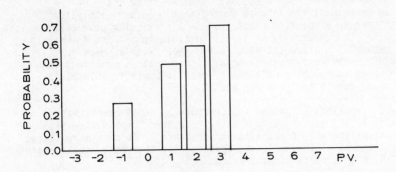

Figure 2.8.   Project 2.

Project 2 E.P.V.

E.P.V. =   -1 x 0.25 + 1 x 0.5 + 2 x 0.6 + 3 x 0.7
E.P.V. =   -0.25 + 0.5 + 1.2 + 2.1
E.P.V. =   +3.55

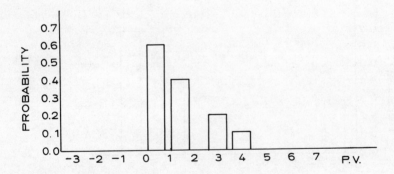

Figure 2.9.   Project 3.

Project 3 E.P.V.

E.P.V. =   0.5 x 0.6 + 1.5 x 0.4 + 3 x 0.2 + 1 x 0.1
E.P.V. =   0.3 + 0.6 + 0.6 + 0.1
E.P.V. =   +1.6

18

By this method the situation shown in Figure 2.7. is superior to those in Figures 2.8. and 2.9. The important factor here is the probability of losing £3 millions and therefore it is doubtful whether an organisation would undertake this risk. The returns on the other two projects are lower but with less risk regarding losses. In Figure 2.8. it shows that there is a small probability of a £1 million loss but again this makes the project a doubtful under-taking. The lowest return is shown for Project 3, Figure 2.9., at £1.6 millions but possibly a conservative type of management would make the decision to embark on this project.

Applications

1. DISCO CITY CAR PARK PROJECT

Two projects were being considered by the Disco City council to improve car parking facilities in the city centre. The projects under review were:

1. A multi storey car park for a total of 291 vehicles.

2. An open car park which would accommodate a total of 150 vehicles.

It was decided that two separate committees would estimate the costs involved and on completion these would be presented to the city's financial consultant for analysis.

In projects of this nature Discounted Cash Flow principles are applied to make comparisons between all the practical alternatives.

In the application of the principles of D.C.F. so far as the Disco City was concerned, the following fundamentals were employed:

(a) The life of the projects were determined over a maximum of twenty-five years. The life is related to the commercial circumstances of the particular project being assessed and if possible a complete physical life cycle of the major component assets is provided for, within the D.C.F. period. It was considered unrealistic to attempt to estimate beyond twenty-five years and in any event discounting beyond that period would result in insignificant present values.

(b) Estimates of outlay together with a year by year spread of expenditure for the proposal and each of the alternatives.

(c) Details of gross receipts on a year by year basis over the project life for each alternative.

(d) Details of expenditure on a year by year basis over the project life for each alternative, to include working expenses, renewals and day to day maintenance.

(e) Each of the year figures under (b) and (d) for each alternative are discounted using the eight per cent discount factors. A comparison of the sum totals for each alternative indicates the project which financially is the best answer to the particular problem, i.e. that showing the greatest Capital Surplus or the smallest Capital Deficit.

It was also the policy that the estimates must be produced, by and large, to include in the calculation of wages a percentage to allow for wage demands over the coming year. For all practical purposes this figure was taken to be eight per cent per annum. However increases in productivity locally tend to decrease the numbers of staff required and therefore this eight per cent increase in wage levels is offset by the following:

For Maintenance staff	4% net,	increase 4%
For Operating staff	3% net,	increase 5%
For other staff	- net,	increase 8%

The committee preparing the report for the open car park were able to consider the following information:

Discount over the period 1978 to 2002. The outlay would be £24,000 in 1978. Consider 260 days car parking per annum.

Receipts would be charged at 25p. per day for the years 1978-80, 50p. for 1981-85 and £1 thereafter.

Expenses would consist of one maintenance wage of £47, plus the four per cent discussed previously for Maintenance staff. This is the yearly amount allocated for the project. Repairs and materials for each year, £63, and electric current £350.

Expenses with barriers on similar sites resulted in costs being allocated as follows:

1. Repairs (contract) £100 per annum.
2. Repairs - materials £80 per annum.

Renewal of the barriers at a cost of £4,000 was scheduled for 1988 and 2000.

The committee preparing the report for the multi storey car park had the following information:

Discount over the period 1978 to 2002. The outlay would be £91,000 in 1978. Consider 260 days per annum car parking.

Receipts would be charged at 25p. per day for the years 1978-80, 50p. for 1981-85 and £1 thereafter.

Expenses would consist of £3,500 per annum allocation for one attendant in 1978, plus four per cent per annum. Allocation of the yearly costs for repairs and materials were obtained from a similar project and are listed as follows:

Year	Repairs and Materials	Year	Repairs and Materials	Year	Repairs and Materials
1979	£140	1987	£240	1995	£140
1980	£170	1988	£170	1996	£200
1981	£175	1989	£140	1997	£140
1982	£170	1990	£170	1998	£170
1983	£140	1991	£175	1999	£140
1984	£170	1992	£170	2000	£170
1985	£140	1993	£140	2001	£270
1986	£200	1994	£170	2002	£170

Electric current was to be charged at £900 per annum.

It was estimated that the car park would require re-surfacing in 1988 at a cost of £2,500.

The renewal of lighting would be necessary in 1990 at a cost of £8,000.

Re-surfacing again would be required in 1998 at £4,000.

Both reports were presented to the Financial Accountant, whose task was to apply D.C.F. to each report and recommend which of the two projects the city should undertake.

Discussion

It was considered by the Committee responsible for setting and estimating prices that, whilst the costs for the open car park were reasonable, those for the multi storey car park were very much on the low side. The following changes were to be made to the calculations.

All calculations for the open car park were to remain as assessed. For the multi storey car park the following would apply: salary for the attendant to be increased by ten per cent for the period 1978-80, by fifteen per cent for 1981-84 and twenty-five per cent thereafter, these being in addition to those calculated.

The cost of re-surfacing to be increased by twenty per cent and lighting by fifty per cent to those already calculated.

Electricity charges to be a total of £1,200, for the period 1978-81, £1,500 for 1982-84 and £2,000 thereafter.

Taking the above costs into consideration for the multi storey car park, what would your recommendation now be?

2. CARANMILK COMPANY LIMITED

The Caranmilk Company Limited were originally manufacturers of car accessories and one of the first companies to design and manufacture seat belts for cars, as a mass produced article. The company took pride in the fact that their very first design was accepted for a safety award and was considered a quality product.

The company had made the decision a few years ago to diversify and had bought a small company on a nearby site. This company operated small milk floats delivering local vegetables, cream and milk to the housewife, and had proved a valuable acquisition. Profits had been good and a fifty per cent expansion of its sales was achieved over a five year period.

A management services department covered the requirements of both divisions of the company in solving financial and production problems.

An immediate problem requiring the attention of management services concerned the evaluation of a new piece of capital equipment, which mass produced seat belts. The machine was expected to have a life of ten years, but with the present rate of technological advance in this area, it was felt that the machine would be obsolete in about three years' time. There were many features of the machine that made the scrap value worth approximately £200,000 in three years' time. The cost of the machine new would be £300,000 and the company's cost of capital was ten per cent.

Three different types of belts were produced to suit various models of cars but the actual production by the machine can be considered as standard and only a slight modification results in three types of belt called Model A, Model B and Model C.

A Market Research Company had been employed to estimate sales of the three types of belt for the next three years. The cost of the survey was £5,000 and the report gave the following information.

Year	Model	Sales of Seat Belts	Probability of Sale
1	A	10,000	0.2
	B	20,000	0.4
	C	30,000	0.4
2	A	10,000	0.1
	B	20,000	0.4
	C	30,000	0.5
3	A	10,000	0.1
	B	20,000	0.3
	C	30,000	0.6

A selling price for all three models of belt for the next three years had been agreed and fixed at £7 each, with the variable costs calculated at £2. The directors of the company were doubtful whether the company should invest in the particular machine. Make your recommendations on the investment.

The second problem under review by management services concerned the division of the company operating the milk floats. The floats each cost £600 to purchase and it was agreed that a financial exercise be carried out, to indicate when the floats should be replaced. Estimates of the annual maintenance charges, together with 'trade in' prices of secondhand floats were found to be:

Age of float (years)	1	2	3	4	5	6
Annual maintenance charge	100	120	140	180	280	300
Estimated trade in price	300	200	100	80	40	---

With this information available it was anticipated that a decision could be made on the number of years the company should operate the milk floats, before replacing with new ones.

Discussion

If, in the problem concerning the seat belts, the cost of capital was increase to twelve per cent and a market research survey showed that the probability of sales for all three models were expected to be reduced by 0.1 for Model A, 0.2 for Model B and Model C over each of the three years, because of increased competition; costs were also expected to increase and although the selling price would remain at £7 the variable costs would be £2.50., what would your recommendation be?

Should the annual maintenance charges rise beyond those stated for the milk floats by twenty-five per cent, as predicted in a report recently received by the management; also, based on the recent report, it was anticipated that the floats would have zero trade in price after year 3, but that the trade in prices for the first three years would remain as stated, would this affect any previous decision as to when to replace the floats?

3. WEST END DISCOUNT STORES

Over many years the stores had experienced problems of staff turnover
and although being an old established family business, no solution
to the problem had been found.

Having completed plans for an extension of the stores on the present
site, the problem of obtaining new staff and staff turnover again
became a serious problem. Regretfully, past experience shows that
sixty per cent of the staff would leave within one year of commencing
employment and only ten per cent would still be with the stores after
two years. It was found from past records of staff that poor canteen
facilities was the major reason for leaving.

After a more detailed study of previous staff turnover figures,
it appeared that of the ten per cent still employed after two years,
none leave in the third year, but all leave at the end of four years.
At the end of each year all the vacancies are filled by employing
new staff.

The West End Discount Stores were well known locally for good rates
of pay and reasonable hours of work. With little prospect of being
able to improve on these conditions, because mainly of government
policy, it was agreed that the leaving rate would be expected to
remain the same for new staff, as for the original 100 employees.

The management of the stores was not convinced that poor canteen
facilities was the reason for the large turnover of staff, but was
willing to accept this reason should informal discussions with
present employees by the Personnel Department show reasonable evidence
of this fact.

The discussions did in fact prove the point that canteen facilities
was a major factor to be considered. It was agreed with the management that the stores would provide £200 towards the improvement of
the staff canteen.

It was estimated that the effect of the canteen improvements would
be to reduce the percentage of employees leaving in the first year
to only forty per cent, but because of other factors the other twenty
per cent who stayed on would leave at the end of the second year
anyway.

Having carefully scrutinised these figures, the management was
uncertain as to whether the £200 to be spent on improving the canteen
facilities would in fact be worthwhile.

The Personnel Department was requested to make a report regarding
the expenditure together with any recommendations. After a costing
exercise, figures showed that it costs on average £20 to recruit
a new member of staff.

For future planning purposes, the Personnel Department was also requested to provide figures on how many staff would end their employment with the stores at the end of three years and four years from the present date. Included in the report should be the expected average number of staff resignations for each year.

Discussion

One of the branch stores has a similar problem, the only difference being that of the probability of sales staff leaving over the four year period. The percentage probability of staff leaving the branch was found to be:

Before canteen improvement		After canteen improvement	
Year 1	40%	Year 1	20%
Year 2	30%	Year 2	30%
Year 3	15%	Year 3	30%
Year 4	15%	Year 4	20%

The Sales Director of the West End Discount Stores stated that there was no need to carry out a costing exercise for the branch stores, as all employees left after four years and all other costs were the same. Would the same conclusion be reached for the branch as that reached for the West End Discount Stores?

4. ELECTRONIC PARTS CO. LTD.

The company had important contracts with the government for specialised metal parts used on advanced weapon developments. The parts
produced were made of a new metal which could be produced by
standard types of equipment, but the result of such production was
the failure of important parts in the producing machines over a
period of time.

The contract with the government included a clause that stated the
responsibility of such failure of standard machines would be borne
by the government if producing this type of equipment. Before any
compensation would be paid the government required evidence that the
best replacement and planned maintenance policies were being observed
and also proof of the number produced on the standard machines.

The management of Electronic Parts could produce evidence of production rates and planned maintenance but a review of the replacement
policy was necessary.

Data collected showed that an important part of the machines under
review was subject to repeated failure and it must be replaced when
the failure occurs. One hundred such machines were being used for
this work.

The cost of individual replacement was £7 per part and for group
replacement the cost was £300 for all the 100 machines. Careful
records have been kept on failure rates over a lengthy period of time
and the distribution of age at failure could be summarised as follows:

If, at the beginning of month 1 there are 100 new parts, then
of these parts:

10 will fail during the 1st month
20 will fail during the 2nd month
30 will fail during the 3rd month
30 will fail during the 4th month
10 will fail during the 5th month

With this data available the best replacement policy that should be
adopted by Electronic Parts Co. Ltd. is required.

Discussion

If the cost of group replacement increased to £400 and individual
replacement cost also increased to £8 per part, how would this affect
the policy?

Assuming the above increases, take into account the following new
failure rates and recommend your replacement policy:

Failure rate in month 1 - 15%
Failure rate in month 2 - 25%
Failure rate in month 3 - 30%
Failure rate in month 4 - 30%

5. PROJECT INVESTMENTS INCORPORATED (P.I.I.)

Three projects were under consideration by Project Investments
Incorporated, but only one would be chosen for capital investment.
Profits expected over a ten year period were carefully calculated
and, within a few thousand poinds, costs for each of the projects
were in the region of £2.45 millions.

Project A

A middle east country recovering from the ravages of war, where
most of the large industrial companies had been destroyed or
badly damaged, was in need of large textile machinery of a
specialised kind.

   The textiles would be protected for a four year period and,
owing to the specialised type of textile produced, the profits
would be considerable for this period, gradually reducing over
the following six years.

   By supplying the equipment, the expected return is shown for
the ten year period in Table 1.

Project B

An Asian country which over the past year or so appeared to have
a more stable government, was in need of a soft drinks factory.
Because of a monopoly situation, the predicted profits should
be consistent over the first five years of its existence, reaching
a peak in year six, but a planned second factory promised to a
certain area of the country would commence supplies in 1985.
This would affect profits considerably from this year onwards.

Project C

In Southern Africa a car assembly plant was required, which was
the final project for consideration. There would be a gradual
build up of production and profits were expected to be low for
the first two years in particular. From year 4 profits should
increase with improved marketing and full production.

   The possibility of increased competition was expected to affect
profits in the final two years being considered.

Table 1

Predicted Profits (£'000s)

Year	Project A	Project B	Project C
1979	220	280	10
1980	350	280	40
1981	500	290	90
1982	390	300	180
1983	180	330	340
1984	120	440	450
1985	90	340	500
1986	80	80	560
1987	70	40	360
1988	70	20	210

Political pressure and the need to invest in the three areas of the world where the projects would be completed because of promises made regarding overseas development, resulted in the Project Investments Incorporated also being under considerable pressure to invest in one of the three projects.

It was agreed that the attractiveness of the three projects varies according to the criteria which are set, but the five different levels of return and the time periods which would be considered, before a final decision was made, were as follows:

(a) Over 10 years @ 8% return
(b) Over 10 years @ 12% return
(c) Over 5 years @ 10% return
(d) Over 5 years @ 12% return
(e) Over 10 years @ 5% return

Although it was expected that one of the projects would be chosen, the final decision as to which would be left to P.I.I.

Which project would you recommend to P.I.I. for investment? State your reasons when giving your report.

Discussion

If you were free from any pressures when considering the projects for investment, what would your recommendations be and what other factors would you consider when making your final report to P.I.I.? Would a higher discounted rate than those considered be more realistic? Consider a discounted rate of 14% for the five alternatives and state your recommendations.

Solutions to applications

1.

DISCO CITY CAR PARK - SUMMARY AND SOLUTION

1. Estimated Outlay

	(a) Multi Storey (291 spaces)	(b) Alternative Ground Level Car Park (150 spaces)
	£	£
Concrete structure, lighting, etc.	91,000	
Levelling and surfacing		20,000
Auto Barrier		4,000
Net Outlay (present value)	91,000	24,000

2. Accounting Allocation

Capital Account Way and Structures Assets	91,000	

3. Spread of Expenditure

Year 1978	91,000	24,000

4. Financial Assessment
   Present values (at 8%) of capital
     surplus of proposal

Net cash flow from operations over
  25 years (after allowing for
  changes in price and wage levels)
	497,314	282,153

DEDUCT net investment to produce annual savings	91,000	24,000
Capital Surplus	406,314	258,153

(Assumes occupation of each space once only per day for 5 days per week.)

PROPOSAL: Select (a) with capital surplus of £406,314 to have
           Multi Storey car park with 291 spaces.

DISCO CITY CAR PARK - MULTI STOREY (291 vehicles, 260 days p.a.)

Year	Outlay £	Receipts £	Wages of Attendant Inc.4%p.a. £	Materials and Repairs £	Electricity £	Renewals £	Total Expenses £	Net Receipts £	8% Discount	P.V. £
1978	91,000									
1979		18,915	3,500	140	900		4,540	14,375	.926	13,311
1980		18,915	3,640	170	900		4,710	14,205	.857	12,174
1981		37,830	3,786	175	900		4,861	32,969	.794	26,177
1982		37,830	3,937	170	900		5,007	32,823	.735	24,125
1983		37,830	4,095	140	900		5,135	32,695	.681	22,265
1984		37,830	4,258	170	900		5,328	32,502	.630	20,476
1985		37,830	4,429	140	900		5,469	32,361	.583	18,866
1986		75,660	4,606	200	900		5,706	69,954	.540	37,775
1987		75,660	4,790	240	900		5,930	69,730	.500	34,865
1988		75,660	4,982	170	900	2,500 (Resurface)	8,552	67,108	.463	31,071
1989		75,660	5,181	140	900		6,221	69,439	.429	29,789
1990		75,660	5,388	170	900	8,000 (Lighting)	14,458	61,202	.397	24,297
1991		75,660	5,603	175	900		6,678	68,982	.368	25,385
1992		75,660	5,828	170	900		6,898	68,762	.340	23,379
1993		75,660	6,061	140	900		7,101	68,559	.315	21,596
1994		75,660	6,303	170	900		7,373	68,287	.292	19,939
1995		75,660	6,555	140	900		7,595	68,065	.270	18,377
1996		75,660	6,818	200	900		7,918	67,742	.250	16,935
1997		75,660	7,090	140	900		8,130	67,530	.232	15,667
1998		75,660	7,374	170	900	4,000 (Resurface)	12,444	63,216	.215	13,591
1999		75,660	7,669	140	900		8,709	66,951	.199	13,323
2000		75,660	7,976	170	900		9,046	66,614	.184	12,256
2001		75,660	8,295	270	900		9,465	66,195	.170	11,253
2002		75,660	8,627	170	900		9,697	65,963	.158	10,422
	91,000	1,513,200	136,791	4,080	21,600	14,500	176,971	1,336,229	-	497,314

Excess of receipts over expenses discounted at 8% for 25 years = £497,314-£91,000 (Investmt) = £406,314 Cap.Surplus

DISCO CITY CAR PARK – Alternative 150 Open Car Spaces (260 days p.a.)

	Outlay £	Receipts £	Repair Wages Inc.4%p.a. £	Expenses Repairs Materials £	Elect- ricity £	Barriers Repairs Contract £	Repairs Materials £	Renewals £	Total Expenses £	Net- Receipts £	8% Discount	P.V. £
1978	24,000											
1979		9,750	47	63	350	100	80		640	9,110	.926	8,436
1980		9,750	49	63	350	100	80		642	9,108	.857	7,805
1981		19,500	51	63	350	100	80		644	18,856	.794	14,971
1982		19,500	53	63	350	100	80		646	18,854	.735	13,857
1983		19,500	55	63	350	100	80		648	18,852	.681	12,838
1984		19,500	57	63	350	100	80		650	18,850	.630	11,875
1985		19,500	60	63	350	100	80		653	18,847	.583	10,988
1986		39,000	62	63	350	100	80		655	38,345	.540	20,706
1987		39,000	64	63	350	100	80		657	38,343	.500	19,171
1988		39,000	67	63	350	100	80	4,000	4,660	34,340	.463	15,899
1989		39,000	70	63	350	100	80		663	38,337	.429	16,446
1990		39,000	72	63	350	100	80		665	38,335	.397	15,219
1991		39,000	75	63	350	100	80		668	38,332	.368	14,106
1992		39,000	78	63	350	100	80		671	38,329	.340	13,032
1993		39,000	81	63	350	100	80		674	38,326	.315	12,073
1994		39,000	85	63	350	100	80		678	38,322	.292	11,190
1995		39,000	88	63	350	100	80		681	38,319	.270	10,346
1996		39,000	92	63	350	100	80		685	38,315	.250	9,578
1997		39,000	95	63	350	100	80		688	38,312	.232	8,888
1998		39,000	99	63	350	100	80		692	38,308	.215	8,236
1999		39,000	103	63	350	100	80		696	38,304	.199	7,622
2000		39,000	107	63	350	100	80	4,000	4,700	34,300	.184	6,311
2001		39,000	111	63	350	100	80		704	38,296	.170	6,510
2002		39,000	116	63	350	100	80		709	38,291	.158	6,050
	24,000	780,000	1,837	1,512	8,400	2,400	1,920	8,000	24,069	755,931	–	282,153

Excess of receipts over expenses discounted @ 8% for 25 years = £282,153-£24,000 (Investmt) = £258,153 Cap.Surplus

2.
CARANMILK COMPANY LIMITED

It is required to find the expected net present value of the project.
The cost of the survey by the Market Research Company of £5,000 is a
sunk cost and therefore does not enter into the analysis.

It is assumed that all the cash flows take place on the last day
of the year.

Expected sales of the seat belts in each year is as follows:

Year 1	Model A	10,000 x 0.2 =	2,000
	Model B	20,000 x 0.4 =	8,000
	Model C	30,000 x 0.4 =	12,000

	Expected sales =	22,000
	£5 contribution per sale	x5
	Total expected contribution	£110,000

Year 2	Model A	10,000 x 0.1 =	1,000
	Model B	20,000 x 0.4 =	8,000
	Model C	30,000 x 0.5 =	15,000

	Expected sales =	24,000
	£5 contribution per sale	x5
	Total expected contribution	£120,000

Year 3	Model A	10,000 x 0.1 =	1,000
	Model B	20,000 x 0.3 =	6,000
	Model C	30,000 x 0.6 =	18,000

	Expected sales =	25,000
	£5 contribution per sale	x5
	Total expected contribution	£125,000

Present value factors at 10%
  from Discount Factor tables

Year 1 =	0.909
Year 2 =	0.826
Year 3 =	0.751

Determining Present Values

Year	Cash Flow	D.C.F. Factor (10%)	P.V.
0	(£300,000)	1.000	(£300,000)
1	110,000	0.909	100,000
2	120,000	0.826	99,174
3	325,000	0.751	244,176

Expected Net Present Value £443,350

Year 3 includes scrap value of £200,000.

Based on these figures the recommendation would be to purchase and undertake the investment.

Milk float problem

The objective is to minimise the average annual cost of the fleet of milk floats. It is necessary to construct a table to show the cumulative maintenance charges and capital outlays. The capital outlay being the difference between the price of a new milk float and the second hand price obtained for the trade in milk float. The maintenance charges and the capital outlay can be summed and then converted to give an annual average cost.

Replacement Age (Years)	Cumulative Maintenance Cost (£)	Capital Outlay (£)	Total Charges (£)	Average Annual Cost (£)
(1)	(2)	(3)	(2) + (3)	$\dfrac{(2) + (3)}{(1)}$
1	100	300	400	400
2	220	400	620	310
3	360	500	860	286.67
4	540	520	1,060	265
5	820	560	1,380	276
6	1,120	600	1,720	286.67

The company should replace the milk floats after four years service.

Proposed solution
3. West End Discount Stores

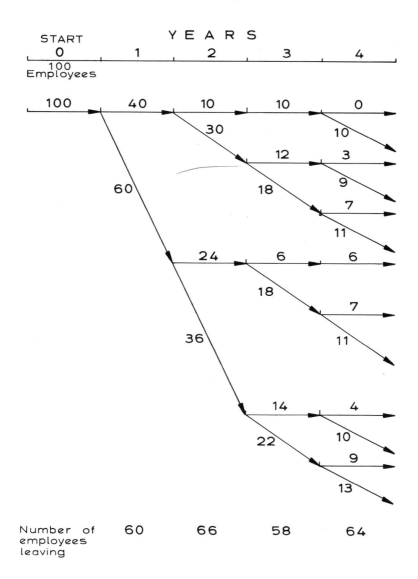

3.

WEST END DISCOUNT STORES

We can see from the tree that commencing with 100 employees (year 0)
the horizontal lines represent the people who stay for the year
being considered and the diagonal line represents those who leave.

In year 1, for example, 60% x 100 = 60 leave and 40 stay. Of the
40 who stay in year 1, 30% x 100 = 30 will leave in year 2, thus
leaving 40-30 = 10 who stay with the stores. Note that the 10 who are
with the stores at the end of year 2 will remain through year 3, but
depart at the end of year 4.

By adding the figures calculated for the diagonals for each year,
we obtain the average number of employees leaving.

At the end of year 3, 18 + 18 + 22 = 58 employees will leave and
therefore require replacing.

At the end of year 4, 10 + 9 + 11 + 11 + 10 + 13 = 64 employees will
leave.

Period of employment in years (x)	Probability of leaving (p)	px
1	0.6	0.6
2	0.3	0.6
3	0.0	0.0
4	0.1	0.4
$\sum p$ = 1.0		$\sum px$ = 1.6 years

Thus the average period of employment for a member of the sales staff
is 1.6 years. As 100 sales staff are employed, the average number of
leavers each year is expected to be:

$$\frac{\text{Total Staff}}{\text{Average length of employment}} = \frac{100}{1.6} = 62.5 \text{ employees}$$

Recruitment costs £20 per person, so that the total annual cost of
replacing lost employees is £20 x £62.5 = £1,250.

If the improvements in canteen facilities are undertaken, the new
mean length of employment will be:

Period of employment in years	Probability of leaving	
(x)	(p)	px
1	0.4	0.4
2	0.5	1.0
3	0.0	0.0
4	0.1	0.4
	$\sum p = 1.0$	$\sum px = 1.8$ years

The average number of staff to be replaced each year will be:

$$\frac{\text{Total Staff}}{\text{Average length of employment}} = \frac{100}{1.8} \approx 56 \text{ employees}$$

The cost of recruitment will be £20 x 56 = £1,120.

The canteen improvements will cost £200 per year and will result in recruitment savings of £1,250 - £1,120 = £130 per year.

The conclusion, on financial grounds only, would be that it is not worthwile improving the facilities of the staff canteen.

4.
ELECTRONIC PARTS CO LTD

The failure rates of the parts are:

Month	Probability (P) that a new part fitted at time zero fails during the month (x)
(x)	(P_x)
1	0.10
2	0.20
3	0.30
4	0.30
5	0.10
	1.00

Calculation of individual replacement

$$10 \times \tfrac{1}{2} = 5$$
$$20 \times 1\tfrac{1}{2} = 30$$
$$30 \times 2\tfrac{1}{2} = 75$$
$$30 \times 3\tfrac{1}{2} = 105$$
$$10 \times 4\tfrac{1}{2} = 45$$
$$260$$

Therefore average life = 2.6 months

Therefore average cost/month = $\dfrac{£700}{2.6}$ = £269

Calculation of group replacement

			Cumulative
$n_0 = n_0$		=100	
$n_1 = n_0 p_1 = 100 \times 0.10$		= 10	10
$n_2 = n_0 p_2 + n_1 p_1 = 100 \times 0.20 + 10 \times 0.10$		= 21	31
$n_3 = n_0 p_3 + n_1 p_2 + n_2 p_1 = 100 \times 0.30 + 10 \times 0.20 + 21 \times 0.30$		= 43	74
$n_4 = n_0 p_4 + n_1 p_3 + n_2 p_2 + n_3 p_1$		= 45	109
$n_5 = n_0 p_5 + n_1 p_4 + n_2 p_3 + n_3 p_2 + n_4 p_1$		= 33	142
$n_6 = \quad n_1 p_5 + n_2 p_4 + n_3 p_3 + n_4 p_2 + n_5 p_1$		= 33	175
$n_7 = \quad\quad n_2 p_5 + n_3 p_4 + n_4 p_3 + n_5 p_2 + n_6 p_1$		= 39	214
$n_8 = \quad\quad\quad n_3 p_5 + n_4 p_4 + n_5 p_3 + n_6 p_2 + n_7 p_1$		= 39	253

Group replacement costs

Interval (months)	Individual Cost						Total Cost	Total Cost per month
1	10 x 7	=	70	+ 300	=		370	370
2	31 x 7	=	217	+ 300	=		517	258
3	74 x 7	=	518	+ 300	=		818	273
4	109 x 7	=	763	+ 300	=		1,063	266
5	142 x 7	=	994	+ 300	=		1,294	259
6	175 x 7	=	1,215	+ 300	=		1,515	253
7	214 x 7	=	1,498	+ 300	=		1,798	257
8	253 x 7	=	1,771	+ 300	=		2,071	259

Conclusion: Group replace at 6 months.

5.
PROJECT INVESTMENTS CORPORATION

Years	Predicted Profits £'000s Projects			P.V. Discounted at 8% (a)			P.V. Discounted at 12% (b)			P.V. Discounted at 5% (e)		
	A	B	C	A	B	C	A	B	C	A	B	C
1979	220	280	10	204	260	9	197	250	9	210	257	9
1980	350	280	40	324	260	37	280	224	32	318	254	25
1981	500	290	90	464	269	83	356	207	64	433	251	78
1982	390	300	180	362	278	167	248	191	115	321	247	148
1983	180	330	340	167	306	315	102	187	193	141	259	267
1984	120	440	450	112	407	377	61	224	229	90	328	336
1985	90	340	500	83	315	464	46	173	254	64	242	355
1986	80	80	560	74	74	519	32	32	226	54	54	380
1987	70	40	360	65	37	334	25	15	130	45	26	232
1988	70	20	210	65	19	195	23	7	68	43	12	129
Total				1,920	2,225	2,500	1,370	1,510	1,320	1,719	1,930	1,959

Decision:
(a) Choose project C over the 10 year period discounted at 8%.
(b) Choose project B over the 10 year period discounted at 12%.
(e) Choose project C over the 10 year period discounted at 5%.

Predicted Profits £'000s

Years	Projects			P.V. Discounted at 10% (c)			P.V. Discounted at 12% (d)		
	A	B	C	A	B	C	A	B	C
1979	220	280	10	200	255	9	197	250	9
1980	350	280	40	289	231	33	280	224	32
1981	500	290	90	376	218	68	356	207	64
1982	390	300	180	266	205	123	248	191	115
1983	180	330	340	112	205	211	102	187	193
Total				1,243	1,114	444	1,183	1,059	413

Decision:
(c) Choose project A over the 5 year period discounted at 10%.
(d) Choose project A over the 5 year period discounted at 12%.

Conclusion:

The attractiveness of the three alternatives varies according to the criteria which are set. At constraints of waiting for ten years, project C is the most attractive, but at the lower discounted rate. Most likely, on the small difference between projects C and B, project B would be chosen, which also has the higher average return rate at 12%.

For the shorter period being considered project A would be chosen.

41

3 Decision trees

The decision tree is a different way of presenting the same information shown in the pay-off table. As the problems become more
complex it presents a more lucid way of presenting the information
than is possible in the pay-off table. By the introduction of a
problem the decision tree method of approach will be presented.

EXAMPLE 1

A company is involved in drilling for oil in the sea, off the coast
of a West African country. The company has been allocated an area
with the option to drill but this will expire in twelve weeks if the
option is not taken up. It would be offered to another company if
the decision is made not to drill. Recent failures to find oil in
'commercial quantities' has reduced the company's liquid assets to
$13 millions.

Three possible choices are open to the company:

1. Let the allocation and offer to drill expire.
2. Drill within twelve weeks.
3. Pay specialist test drillers for a test run. Depending on the
   results of the test, decide whether to undertake drilling or not.

Careful analysis of the geology of the sea bed shows that there is a
probability of 0.60 that should the company drill they would find oil
of the required grade. In drilling similar types of areas the
company finds that if a test drill shows favourable signs of oil then
a probability of 0.90 can be applied, that oil would be found if the
company undertook commercial drilling operations. Should the test
not prove satisfactory then past experience would warrant only a
probability of 0.10 that oil would be found if a decision to drill
was made.

   In assessing the probability that a test drill, if made, would show
favourable signs of oil, past experience shows that a probability of
0.65 could be applied.

   Within the time possible for a test drill to be made, this can be
done for $95,000. The cost of commercial drilling from a platform
would be $1.5 millions. Because of the political situation, the
company will not keep the oil rights if oil is found, but the African
government would offer $4 millions for these rights irrespective of
the quality of the oil and possible reserves.

   A decision tree is made up of a series of nodes and branches. The
decision points are denoted by a square and chance events by circles.
Other symbols can and are used, but these two symbols will be

42

adhered to throughout the chapter. The tree will always show a combination of (a) decision choices, with (b) different possible events or results of decisions which are partially affected by chance or other uncontrollable circumstances. It is not always possible to identify all the events that can happen or all the decisions one has to make. Therefore it is only possible to present those decisions and events that are considered important and have consequences one wishes to compare.

Figure 3.1. shows the decision tree for the problem. At the first node on the left the company has the choice whether to make a drilling test or not. Each branch represents an alternative course of action or decision. If a drilling test is made, from a further node there is a chance event whether the test is satisfactory or unsatisfactory. Following this chance event a decision needs to be made whether or not to drill.

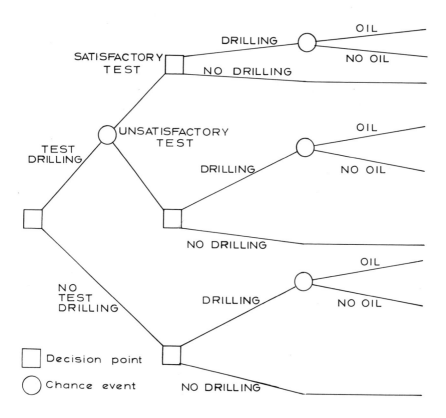

Figure 3.1. Oil company's decision problem

43

Should a decision be made not to make a test drill a further
decision is necessary whether to drill commercially or avoid this
undertaking. This is shown in the lower branches of Figure 3.1.
The possible choices open to the company have been portrayed and
necessary additions are the probabilities and economic consequences
of any decision made.

In Figure 3.2. the probabilities have been applied and the cash flow
shown. The cash flow associated with each decision is shown as a
negative value if associated with costs and considered as an outflow
of money. A positive value is shown if an inflow of cash to the
company or available liquid assets exist.

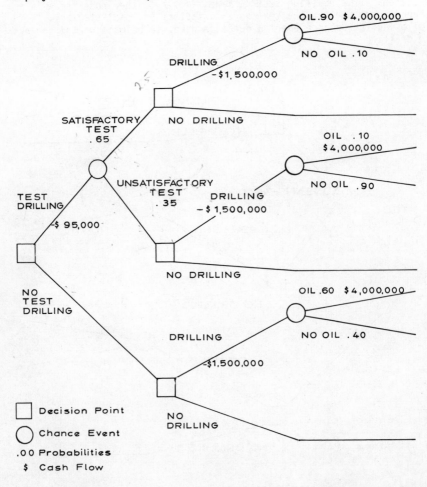

Figure 3.2. Decision tree design with probabilities and cash flows.

Depending on the problem, the objective may be to follow a course of action to consider costs, profits or net cash flows, but in this instance the company requires the best course of action so that the net liquid assets are at a maximum. Therefore we wish to maximise the mathematical expectation of the asset position. We proceed in the following manner:

1. Find the company's asset position at the end of each of the nine branches.

2. Proceed to determine the best course of action for the company by 'rolling back' from the nine branches, i.e. from right to left through the tree. At each fork which joins at a chance event compute the expected value and also at each decision fork. Choose the action that will give the highest expected value.

Calculating the asset position.

The cash flow figures shown in Figure 3.2. consist of -$95,000 for test drilling and -$1.5 millions for commercial drilling. The figure of $4 millions is the net inflow, if oil is found.

We are now ready for the next stage in the analysis - to compare the consequences of different courses of action. All available information has been laid out to give a pictorial view of the alternatives available. The decision tree does not give management the answer to an investment problem but assists in determining which alternative at any particular choice point will yield the greatest expected monetary gain. The gains, of course, must be viewed with the risks.

At the end of each of the nine branches in Figure 3.3. is the asset position of the company following the nine possible courses of action. The calculation for the top branch is as follows:

Company's present assets	$13,000,000
Asset inflow if oil found	$ 4,000,000
Total	$17,000,000
Less both drilling costs	$ 1,595,000
Total	$15,405,000

We can reduce the above total by $4 millions for the second branch if no oil is found giving a figure of $11,405,000. 'Rolling back' to the terminal forks we can calculate the expected values of the company's assets at each of the three points. Each calculation is a weighted average of each of the numbers at the end of the forks. If we take the top fork the calculation would be ($15,405,000 x 0.90 + $11,405,000 x 0.10) which equals $15,004,000. This is entered at the terminal of the forks in Figure 3.3. The assumption is made that the company would accept $15,004,000 certain asset position in exchange for a 90% probability of $15,405,000 plus a 10% probability of $11,405,000. On the same basis, calculations for the remaining two terminals are made, these being $11,805,000 and $13,900,000 respectively.

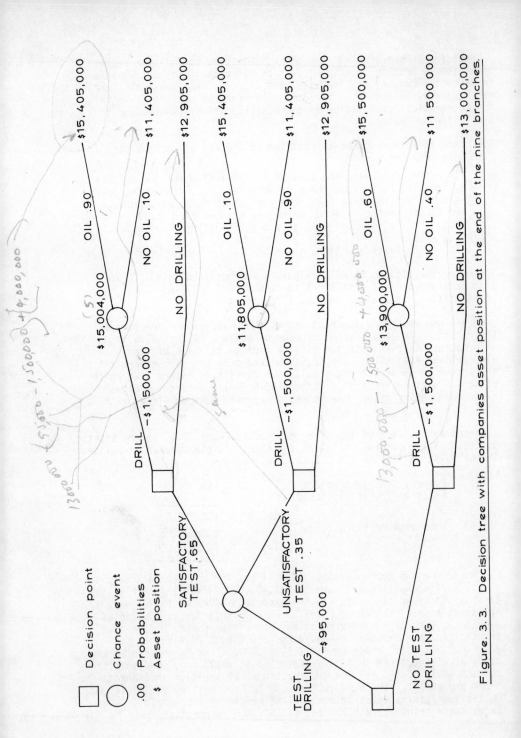

Figure. 3.3. Decision tree with companies asset position at the end of the nine branches.

Legend:
- ☐ Decision point
- ◯ Chance event
- .00 Probabilities
- $ Asset position

Branches:

TEST DRILLING −$95,000

SATISFACTORY TEST .65
DRILL −$1,500,000
$15,004,000
OIL .90 → $15,405,000
NO OIL .10 → $11,405,000
NO DRILLING → $12,905,000

UNSATISFACTORY TEST .35
DRILL −$1,500,000
$11,805,000
OIL .10 → $15,405,000
NO OIL .90 → $11,405,000
NO DRILLING → $12,905,000

NO TEST DRILLING
DRILL −$1,500,000
$13,900,000
OIL .60 → $15,500,000
NO OIL .40 → $11,500,000
NO DRILLING → $13,000,000

46

We now have a value at the terminals of each of the three chance
event forks, which is equivalent to the mathematical expectations of
the two branches, therefore these branches can be removed and a new
statement decision tree can be formed as Figure 3.4.

The company now has a straightforward decision to make if it
decides to test drill, for example, and if the test is satisfactory,
whether or not to drill commercially. It would choose the branch
having the highest mathematical expectation which would be to drill,
as the value of $15,004,000 is superior to $12,905,000 for no drilling.
Should the company decide to test drill and the test prove to be
unsatisfactory, then a decision of no commercial drilling would be
made as the mathematical expectation of $12,905,000 is higher than
drilling at $11,805,000.

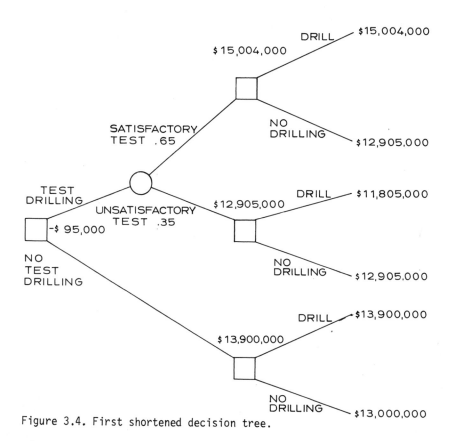

Figure 3.4. First shortened decision tree.

The same reasoning applies to the lower course of action, that of no test drilling. Here we would choose to drill, as the figure of $13,900,000 is a higher value than $13,000,000.

To roll back further and obtain a second reduction of the decision tree, shown in Figure 3.5., we have a terminal of a chance event relating to the results of the test drilling. The procedure is the same as adopted for the previous terminal. We will take the mathematical expectation (ME) of the numbers at the end of the branches thus:

ME = ($15,004,000 x 0.65 + $12,905,000 x 0.35)
ME = $9,752,925 + $4,516,750
ME = $14,269,675

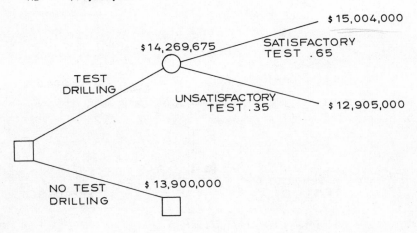

Figure 3.5. Second shortened decision tree.

By 'rolling back' to the start we can now make our decision whether or not we should make a test drilling and the course of action to be taken. The figure at the event terminal at the top of the decision tree in Figure 3.5. shows $14,269,675 for test drilling and it is this decision the company should take. This is a higher mathematical expectation than for no test drilling, showing a figure of $13,900,000. The final decision tree is shown in Figure 3.6.

To avoid any unnecessary complications a comparatively simple example has been introduced. Like any other management technique, it can be misused and certain dangers exist. The decision tree requires skillful construction to avoid complexity but at the same time present the true problem. The use of experts will often be required except for the simple type of tree.

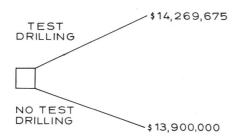

TEST
DRILLING — $14,269,675

NO TEST
DRILLING — $13,900,000

Figure 3.6. Final shortened decision tree.

One of the unique features of the decision tree is that it allows management to combine analytical techniques such as discounted cash flow (discussed in another chapter) and present value methods with a clear picture of the impact of future decision alternatives and events. By using the decision tree management can consider various courses of action with greater ease and clarity.

The method should be looked upon as a further guide to decision making.

To analyse a tree the relevant information must be obtained, quantified and assembled as in other techniques. In many businesses a considerable amount of information used cannot easily have probabilities attached to it, but this is where management must carefully analyse and use the necessary judgement required. The decision tree forces the actual estimates made to be written down for each separate portion of the tree where it can be presented, discussed and reviewed by others.

49

EXERCISES

1. A large European consortium has owned land in a West African
   country for many years awaiting permission for exploration of
   minerals. Permission has recently been granted to dig, but should
   the company decide not to undertake this work an offer from the
   Ministry of Natural Resources to purchase the land for $6 millions
   has been made.

   The company know from previous tests that the mineral exists
   but are unsure of the yields, which are considered in three
   categories, high, medium or low. The company put the probability
   of such yields as ·20, ·30 and ·40 respectively. The expected life
   of the mine is considered to be very short.

   Because of the fluctuation in prices for such a mineral there
   are three basic choices available whether the yields be high,
   medium or low. The company can decide to sell as it is mined,
   store and place on the market in one year's time, or offer for
   sale in two years' time. This procedure is often adopted because
   of price differences and production rates elsewhere in the world.

   The problems of costs, inflation and present worth have been
   taken into consideration in estimating the returns in $ of such
   decisions. The probabilities of obtaining the returns and
   estimated returns for each decision is shown in the following
   table.

Yield	Decision	Probability	$ Returns
High	Sell now	.85	3,000,000
	Sell in 1 year	.75	3,500,000
	Sell in 2 years	.65	4,000,000
Medium	Sell now	.90	2,800,000
	Sell in 1 year	.80	3,000,000
	Sell in 2 years	.65	3,200,000
Low	Sell now	.90	2,600,000
	Sell in 1 year	.80	2,900,000
	Sell in 2 years	.70	3,100,000

   The company wishes to maximise its returns, what recommendations
   should be made to the company?

2. A company has for many years been very successful in marketing
an electrical appliance for household cleaning. It had been
suggested for some time by certain members of the management
board that a new design of the appliance be undertaken. Other
members had proposed that certain modifications only need be
made. There was also a proposal that the present model be
continued without any change because of its successful sales
record.

   A market survey had been carried out to find the reaction to
a new model, a model with modifications and the present model.
The results of this survey were classified as 'high acceptability'
or 'low acceptability' to the three proposals.

   For each of the results from the survey the company needs to
make a decision on three rates of production, high, medium or
low.

   At the present time the main concern of the company was that
costs should be kept as low as possible. Costs and probabilities
relating to the problem are shown in the following table.

Project	Survey Result	Probab- ility	Probabilities of Production		Yearly Costs (£'000,000)	
Develop new model	High acceptability	0.7	High Medium Low	0.9 0.8 0.5	High Medium Low	2 3 5
Develop new model	Low acceptability	0.3	High Medium Low	0.4 0.7 0.9	High Medium Low	2 3 5
Modification	High acceptability	0.75	High Medium Low	0.95 0.8 0.6	High Medium Low	1.5 2.5 4
Modification	Low acceptability	0.25	High Medium Low	0.5 0.7 0.9	High Medium Low	1.5 2.5 4
Continue present design					High	7.5

   The company has found in the past that, although surveys give an
indication of the public reaction to new models they have been
proven wrong on a number of occasions. This has been taken into
consideration when deriving the probabilities of production rates.

   Whichever production rate is chosen the company has enough work
to either support the plant or transfer to an adjacent site.

   What decision should the company make to keep costs at a minimum,
which is the criteria set?

51

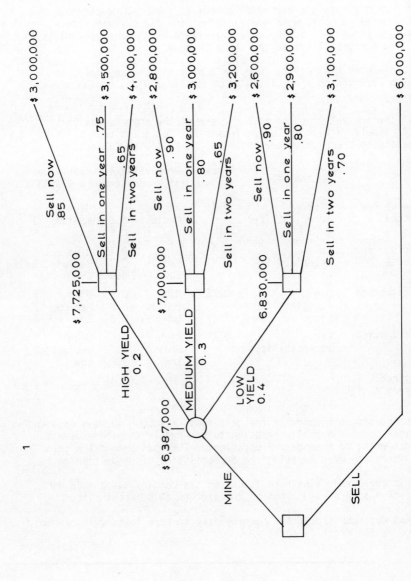

The recommendation would be to mine for the mineral. However, the difference is marginal and many factors require consideration such as whether money received immediately could be invested with a higher rate of return.

2.

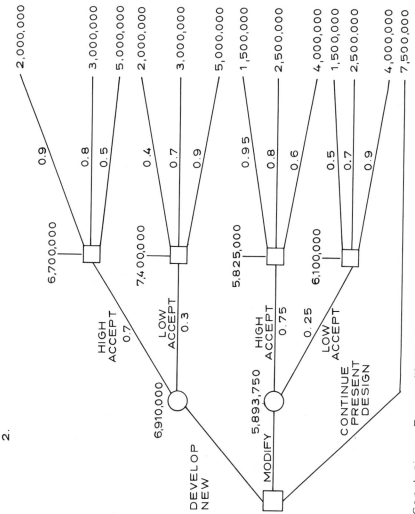

		2,000,000
	0.9	
6,700,000	0.8	3,000,000
HIGH ACCEPT 0.7	0.5	5,000,000
	0.4	2,000,000
7,400,000	0.7	3,000,000
LOW ACCEPT 0.3	0.9	5,000,000
6,910,000	0.95	1,500,000
DEVELOP NEW	0.8	2,500,000
5,825,000	0.6	
HIGH ACCEPT 0.75	0.5	4,000,000
MODIFY 5,893,750	0.7	1,500,000
6,100,000	0.9	2,500,000
LOW ACCEPT 0.25		4,000,000
CONTINUE PRESENT DESIGN		7,500,000

Conclusion: By modifying the present model, the criteria would be met.

53

Applications

1. FISH DISTRIBUTORS LIMITED

A small company on the east coast of England once a week sends its representative to visit to local docks to purchase fish. The visit is always made in the early morning to enable better quality fish to be purchased. The crates of fish are then taken to the premises of Fish Distributors Ltd, where they are allocated to various stores and businesses in the city.

The company has not been happy with its buying policy for some time. The demand for fish has varied considerably over time, which has resulted in fish having to be dumped as it is company policy that, for health reasons, fish not sold the same day is given to animals or thrown away. No profit is made when given to local animal farms.

Estimates of the demand characteristics each day were made and are shown in the following table:

Number of crates	Probability of demand
0	0.05
100	0.15
200	0.45
300	0.30
400	0.05
500 or more	0.00
	1.00

The fish is purchased in standard crates and also sold in the same way. One of the problems, which cannot be altered, is that the purchase of fish must be made in lots of 100, 200, 300 or 400 crates. The cost of each crate is £10 and the current selling price is £12.50.

Three recommendations are required by the company, based on the data presented:

1. The expected value of each alternative purchasing policy.

2. The most probable result of a day's trading if the company decided to purchase loads of 500 crates.

3. The maximum amount Fish Distributors Ltd can afford, or are prepared to pay, to obtain an exact market forecast for the following day.

54

Discussion

A change in marketing conditions has resulted in the demand for fish being increased and probabilities associated with the demand each day are:

Number of crates	Probability of demand
0	0.05
100	0.15
200	0.20
300	0.30
400	0.30
500 or more	0.00
	1.00

With other factors remaining the same, restate your three recommendations.

2. MANAGEMENT SERVICES LIMITED

The authorities of an overseas country had many years ago sanctioned the building of an industrial estate. The object of the project was to encourage firms to consider investing away from the capital city. Incentives were so generous that many firms had in fact developed small industries on the estate. One of the conditions attached to generous loans granted to the various companies was that ninety per cent of the labour employed was to be obtained from a certain area around the estate, and this had been successful in lowering the local unemployment figure.

One such company manufacturing bread and local delicacies had been so successful in its trading that it wished to apply for an expansion licence. Several problems existed however, including the necessity of obtaining a loan for the expansion, and also local politics. An election locally was due within the next two years and the forecast of demand for the produce was uncertain beyond the next year.

The company wished to discuss the problem with the authority concerned and also requested the assistance of a management services expert who could be made available, if required, by the government.

After careful consideration by the expert, company and local authority, three policies were considered possible.

1. Build adjacent to the existing plant a LARGE NEW PLANT.

2. Build adjacent to the existing plant a SMALL NEW PLANT.

3. Build adjacent to the existing plant a small new plant and EXPAND AFTER TWO YEARS if the demand justifies it.

It was necessary to obtain data in the areas of EXPECTED DEMAND, ANNUAL INCOMES and CAPITAL COSTS so that by some method it would be possible to decide which of the three policies to adopt.

A study group was formed which included the management services expert, the local authority and representatives of the company concerned.

Expected demand

Forecasts were made for future demand and it was decided to attach a probability factor to each possibility. As with any forecast, no one can be certain and only by careful examination of past figures combined with experience can the future trend be obtained. The following three possibilities were available to the group.

	Probability
1. Expected demand initially high (2 years) and sustained high	60%
2. Expected demand initially high (2 years) and long term low	10%
3. Expected demand initially low, continuing low	30%

If after two years demand was such that an expansion was justified, then it was estimated that the probabilities for future expected demand over the next eight years would be:

	Probability
sustained high	0.86
long term low	0.14

After the two year period a decision to expand or not expand requires to be made.

Annual incomes

After careful analysis the annual cash flow was obtained for the various possibilities being considered.

1. A large plant with a high sustained demand £100,000

2. A large plant with a low market volume £ 10,000

3. A small plant during the first two years' high demand £ 45,000
Dropping to £25,000 with a sustained high demand,
due to competition from other manufacturers.

4. A small plant expanded after two years with high
sustained demand over remaining eight years £ 70,000

5. A small plant expanded after two years but the
high demand not sustained £ 5,000

6. A small plant with low market demand £ 40,000

The above figures are annual cash flows.

Capital costs

To complete the necessary collection of data all capital costs were estimated and entered into three categories:

1. Large plant £300,000

2. Small plant £130,000

3 Expansion of small plant after two years £220,000

With all the data collected, there were various alternative methods for assessing which policy would be the best to implement. It was decided to analyse the problem using a decision tree method and observe the expected monetary values for the policies. The second method would be to set up a payoff matrix and show which policy gives the maximum 'safe' profit for our consideration.

Finally, it would be advisable to study the difference between the two approaches and then indicate the way in which discounting the cash flows (D.C.F.) would affect the decisions.

Discussion

After a re-examination of the project, the probabilities were
considered correct, but a careful analysis of the annual cash flows
resulted in the following changes.

1. A large plant with a high sustained demand   £120,000

2. A large plant with a low market volume   £ 15,000

3. A small plant during the first two years' high demand £ 45,000
   This dropping to £40,000 with a sustained high demand
   due to competition from other manufacturers.

4. A small plant expanded after two years with high
   sustained demand over remaining eight years   £ 70,000

5. A small plant expanded after two years but the
   high demand not sustained   £ 5,000

6. A small plant with low market demand   £ 40,000

Review your conclusions using the new information that has become
available. All other factors remaining the same as in the original
problem.

Solutions to applications

1.
FISH DISTRIBUTORS LIMITED

1. Purchasing policies:

Purchase policy	Expected profit (£)
Buy 0 crates	0
Buy 100 crates	187.5
Buy 200 crates	187.5
Buy 300 crates	0
Buy 400 crates	0

2. The most probable outcome if the company purchases 500 crates would be a loss of £2,500.

3. Over the period of 100 days, opting for the policy of purchasing either 100 or 200 crates would produce profits of £18,750.

Profit over 100 days, knowing the exact demand:

```
 5 days @ £  0   = £      0
15 days @ £250   = £  3,750
45 days @ £500   = £ 22,500
30 days @ £750   = £ 22,500
 5 days @ £1,000 = £  5,000
                   ─────────
                   £53,750
                   ─────────
```

The difference between policy recommended with profits of £18,750 and profits knowing exact demand of £53,750 is £53,750 - £18,750 = £35,000. Therefore Fish Distributors Limited could afford to pay up to £350 per day.

1. FISH DISTRIBUTORS LIMITED

BUY 0. COST £0 — SELL NONE OR MORE PROBABILITY 1.0 — £0.

BUY 100. COST £1000 — £1187.5
- SELL NONE — PROBABILITY — 0.05 — £0.
- SELL 100 OR MORE — 0.95 — £1250

BUY 200 COST £2000 — £2187.5
- SELL NONE — 0.05 — £0.
- SELL 100 — 0.15 — £1250
- SELL 200 OR MORE — 0.8 — £2500

BUY 300 COST £3000 — £2625
- SELL NONE — 0.05 — £0.
- SELL 100 — 0.15 — £1250
- SELL 200 — 0.45 — £2500
- SELL 300 OR MORE — 0.35 — £3750

BUY 400 COST 4000 — £2687.5
- SELL NONE — 0.05 — £0.
- SELL 100 — 0.15 — £1250
- SELL 200 — 0.45 — £2500
- SELL 300 — 0.30 — £3750
- SELL 400 — 0.05 — £5000

BUY 500 COST £5000 — 'MOST PROBABLY' SELL 200 — £2500

1. PURCHASING POLICIES

60

2. MANAGEMENT SERVICES LIMITED

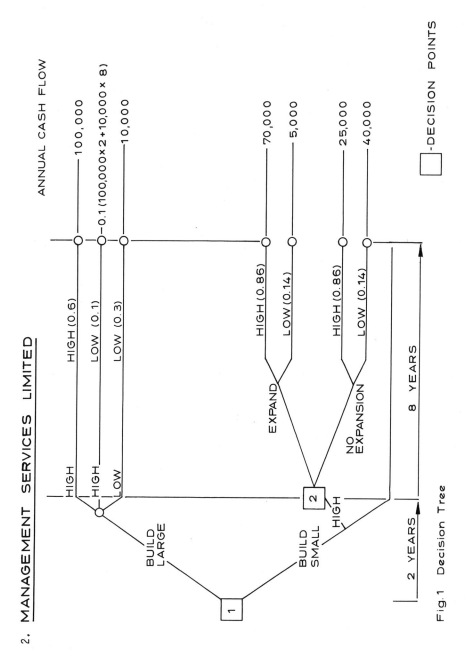

Fig.1 Decision Tree

61

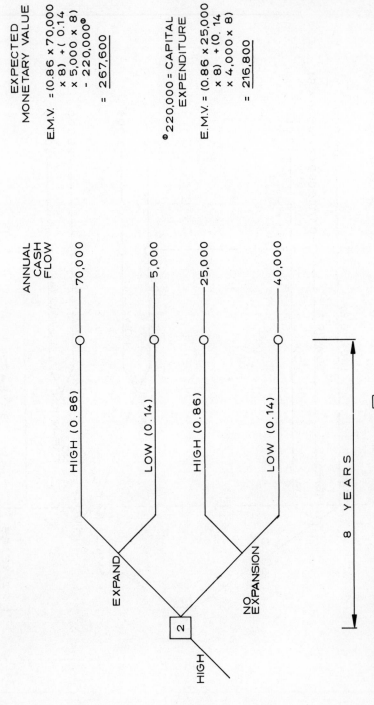

Fig. 2 Consider from Decision point 2

MANAGEMENT SERVICES LIMITED

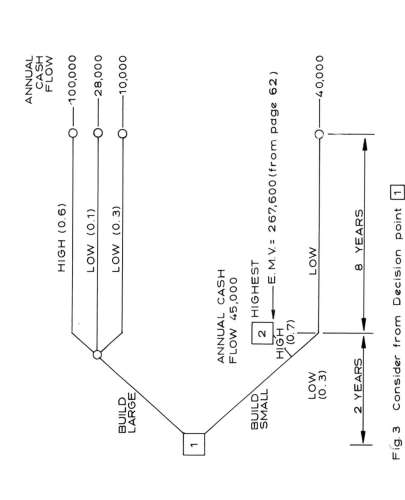

EXPECTED
MONETARY VALUE

E.M.V. = (0.6 × 100,000
× 10) + (0.3
× 10,000 × 10)
+ 0.1 (100,000
× 2 + 10,000
× 8) – 300,000

= 358,000

ANNUAL
CASH
FLOW

HIGH (0.6) ——————100,000

LOW (0.1) ——————28,000

LOW (0.3) ——————10,000

ANNUAL CASH
FLOW 45,000

[2] HIGHEST
    E.M.V. = 267,600 (from page 62)

HIGH
(0.7)

LOW ——————40,000

LOW
(0.3)

E.M.V. = (0.7 ×
45,000 × 2)
+ (0.3 ×
40,000 × 10)
– 120,000

= 240,000

HIGHEST E.M.V.
= BUILD LARGE
  INITIALLY

BUILD
LARGE

BUILD
SMALL

[1]

2 YEARS   8 YEARS

Fig. 3   Consider from Decision point [1]

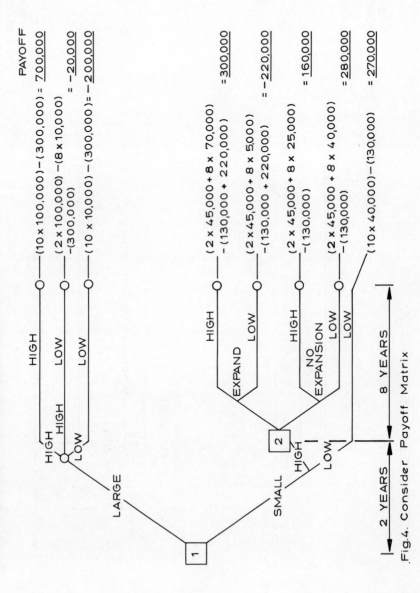

MANAGEMENT SERVICES LIMITED

PAYOFF

HIGH —— (10 x 100,000) – (300,000) = 700,000

LOW —— (2 x 100,000) – (8 x 10,000) = – 20,000
          – (300,000)

LOW —— (10 x 10,000) – (300,000) = – 200,000

HIGH —— (2 x 45,000 + 8 x 70,000) = 300,000
          – (130,000 + 220,000)

EXPAND LOW —— (2 x 45,000 + 8 x 5,000) = – 220,000
                – (130,000 + 220,000)

HIGH —— (2 x 45,000 + 8 x 25,000) = 160,000
          – (130,000)

NO
EXPANSION LOW —— (2 x 45,000 + 8 x 40,000) = 280,000
                  – (130,000)

LOW —— (10 x 40,000) – (130,000) = 270,000

2 YEARS   8 YEARS

Fig.4. Consider Payoff Matrix

64

Consider pay off matrix (continued)

Action	State of Outcome '000s			Minimum of Row	Maximum Figure of Low Minimums
	High	High --- Low	Low		
Build large	700	-20	-200	-200	
Build small then expand	300	-220		-220	
Build small but no expansion	160	280	270	160	160*

Policy build small with no expansion. *'Guarantees' profit of at least £160,000 with no risk of loss.

Conclusion

The method of E.M.V. gives maximum return if forecasts of probabilities are correct but it incurs a risk of loss £200,000 if the demand stays low.

The Maxmin payoff approach policy avoids such a risk but results in a smaller profit.

D.C.F. would favour the 'build small' policy as cash expenditures are delayed.

The final optimum policy depends on the discounting of each year's cash flow.

4   Network planning

Network planning has many names associated with it such as critical path analysis and critical path method, however the difference between them is marginal and network planning will be referred to in this chapter.

Network planning was born of a need to deal with inevitably growing complexity in project work, resulting from rapid advances in technology as well as a multiplication of functional responsibilities. It is no longer possible for managers and engineers to plan and control projects by experience alone or work in an independent way. Project situations must be defined more clearly so that the factors impinging on those situations are understood before any major work is undertaken. Network planning is essentially a basis for doing just this and indeed for coordinating and controlling project work more efficiently.

A network is a diagrammatic plan, drawn up by using the three basic symbols given below to express in logical form the many interconnected relationships of activities involved in carrying out a project.

An arrow represents an ACTIVITY

This is a job of work which takes time and resources. The arrow usually points left to right but is not drawn to any time scale. The head of the arrow conventionally indicates where the job ends, but the length of the arrow is purely for geometric convenience.

A small circle or 'node' represents an EVENT

This is a point in time or intersection at which activities can start or finish. The event circle has a reference number in it.

Each activity starts and finishes with an event. The arrows are joined together to show the logical relationship between activities. In the following example B depends on activity A, or activity B can only be started when activity A is completed.

To show that activities A and B are independent of each other it would be shown thus:

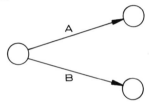

A dotted line represents a DUMMY activity

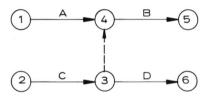

This is used only to show clear logical dependencies between certain activities and it is entirely divorced from time and resource considerations.

An activity cannot start until the event preceding it has occurred. An event cannot occur until all activities leading to it are complete.

To combine activities that are dependent, independent and the use of a dummy, a simple example will suffice:

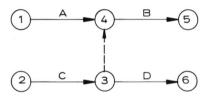

In this network the logic states that activity B depends upon A and C but independent of D. Activity D depends only on C. Thus event 4 cannot occur until event 3 has occurred. The direction of the dummy is of vital importance. The numbers in the circles are bigger at the head of the activity than the tail.

TAIL EVENT ... HEAD EVENT

A project can be defined as some complex operation which has both a definite start and a definite finish stage, we should therefore conventionally have only ONE event point both at the beginning and end of our diagram.

Initially, when drawing a network the time factor is ignored, so that planning attention can be concentrated on how activities are logically related irrespective of how long any one activity will take. Logic first. Timing afterwards.

Having satisfactorily completed the logic diagram or network, the next step is to add estimates of the duration time of each activity to the network. An analysis can then be made to find out how long the project will take and at what time each event will be reached.

It is good practice to redraw the circles or nodes so that the Earliest Event Times and Latest Event Times can be added to the event reference number thus:

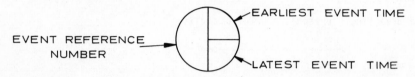

EVENT REFERENCE NUMBER

EARLIEST EVENT TIME

LATEST EVENT TIME

EXAMPLE 1

Draw the network for the following project containing eight activities.

A and C are the start activities. B and D follow A and C respectively but all four activities must be completed before G starts. E comes after C and F after E. Activities E and F are overlapped with D and G. When activities A, B, C, D, E, F and G are completed, the final activity H can begin.

Activity:		Duration (days):	
	A		3
	B		5
	C		4
	D		3
	E		6
	F		8
	G		15
	H		10

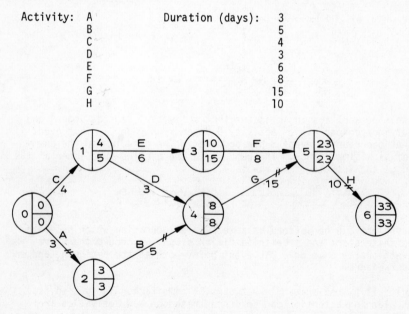

Figure 4.1. Network for example 1 with time analysis.

68

To analyse the network using the activity times given, first assume that the starting event occurs at zero time and then ADD the activity times from this event systematically forward through the network. Where two or more activities lead into an event, the HIGHEST number is selected as this represents the longest time path from the starting event. This gives all the earliest event times. Now assume that the earliest event time at the FINAL event is the same as the latest event time and then work back through the network SUBTRACTING the activity times from the latest event times. Where two or more activity tails originate at an event the LOWEST number is selected, as this represents the longest path back to the final event. This gives all the latest event times.

If we analyse Figure 4.1. further, the total project time is 33 days and the longest path through the network is 0-2-4-5-6 or activities A, B, G and H, these being the critical activities. The network is actually communicating that activity A must start at 0 and be complete at 3, B must commence immediately afterwards at 3 and finish at 8, activity G commence at 8 completed by 23 and the final activity started at 23, and finally completed by 33. All this must be done if the project is to be complete by day 33. These are the critical activities and thus the critical path through the network.

The critical activities are marked thus:

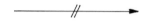

CALCULATION OF FLOATS

By observing any critical activity in the example given, one can see that the difference between the times at the head event and tail event are equal to the duration time of the activity. There is, therefore, no 'spare' time available, or what is called 'float' on any critical activity. A definition of a critical activity could therefore be: any activity that has zero floats. There are three float times to be calculated: Total, Free and Independent.

1)Total float

Taking activity F from our example:

Total float = latest time head event - earliest time tail event
             - duration
  Total float = 23 - 10 - 8 = 5

This calculation gives an indication of time available, but should all this time be utilised on one activity it can affect the total float available on other activities. The reader can check this by calculating total float times for other activities and observe the effect it has.

② Free float

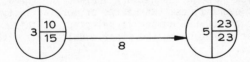

    Free float = earliest time head event - earliest time tail event
                        - duration
    Free float = 23 - 10 - 8 = 5

The calculation happens to be as shown for the total float but this need not be so. The figure is the amount of time the activity can be delayed from the earliest time at the tail event without affecting the earliest time at the head event. In this example:

    10 + 5 delay + duration time of 8 = 23.

③ Independent float

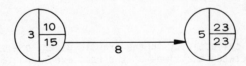

    Independent float = earliest time head event - latest time tail event
                          - duration
    Independent float = 23 - 15 - 8 = 0

This calculation gives the amount of time the activity can be delayed without affecting any other activity. This is perhaps the most important float calculation. For this activity there is zero float, but the reader can practise these calculations with the problems offered at the end of the chapter and observe that other values obviously will exist.

As it is not possible to have negative time, should a calculation give a negative value this should be considered as zero float time.

Float has two important uses

    1. As an indicator of the relative importance of an activity to
       the timing of the project. The more float there is available

the less importance that activity has to the whole time for the project. Note again that a critical activity obviously has zero float.

2. As a means of allowing delay or extension of time for scheduling, especially to allow better use of limited resources.

EXAMPLE 2.

In our example 1 the overall project time is 33 days and we have used 'normal' duration times for the activities. This means the times agreed, without the use of extra overtime, men or machines. Therefore in considering costs for the first time, normal costs are incurred with normal duration times. A further time for each activity can be calculated, that of 'crashing'. This implies that no costs have been spared to obtain the reduced time, e.g. weekend work, overtime, etc. The rise in costs for crashing is likely to be different for each activity. If we have to consider shortening a project by accelerating some of the critical activities we should first select those activities which would cost least to speed up.

Additional data has been made available to our previous example 1:

Activity	Normal Duration (days)	Total Cost (£)	Crash Duration (days)	Crash Total Cost (£)	Cost/Day (£)
A	3	60	-	-	-
B	5	100	4	120	20
C	4	80	-	-	-
D	3	80	2	150	70
E	6	150	5	180	30
F	8	160	-	-	-
G	15	300	10	400	20
H	10	200	8	290	45
		£1,130			

With this additional information, the optimum duration time and cost is required. Previous calculations show that the normal duration time for the project is 33 days at a cost of £1,130, calculated above.

We only need to consider those activities on the critical path to reduce the overall project time and it is to our advantage to consider those with the least cost first.

Activity G with a saving of 5 days at £20 per day would reduce the project completion time 33 - 5 = 28 days at a cost of £1,130 + (£5 x £20) = £1,230. Can this be improved?

The network redrawn would be:

71

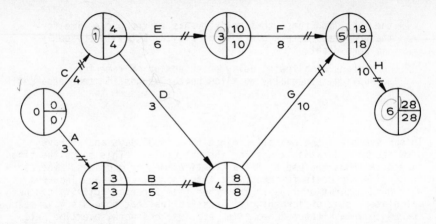

Figure 4.2. First reduction in project time.

Activity B with costs of £20 per day, saving 1 day, is possible but path 0 - 1 - 3 - 5 - 6 would still be critical at 28 days, therefore we must also consider a further activity on this path if we are to reduce 28 days. The activity on this path with least cost is E at £30 per day. By combining the costs of both those activities we can reduce the overall project time to 28 - 1 = 27 days at a cost of £1,230 + (£30 + £20) = £1,280. The network should now show the following position:

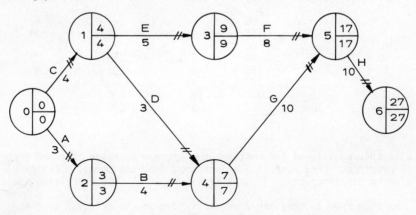

Figure 4.3. Second reduction in project time.

Can we improve on the overall project time? The next lowest cost is for activity H at £45 per day and a possible saving of 2 days. This would reduce the project time to 27 - 2 = 25 days at a cost of £1,280 + (2 x £45) = £1,370. The network, Figure 4.4., now shows the following position:

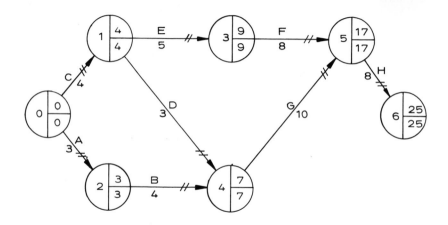

Figure 4.4. Third and final reduction in project time.

Only one further activity can be considered for reduction, that is D at £70 per day, but no saving in time would be possible as both paths 0 - 2 - 4 - 5 - 6 and 0 - 1 - 3 - 5 - 6 result in the project time being 25 days. Thus the optimum time is 25 days at a total cost of £1,370.

EXAMPLE 3.

If in the previous example 2 a customer desired the completion of the project earlier than normal and offered £40 per day bonus for every day saved, would the solution calculated still apply?

Activity G would still be considered first saving 5 days, but the costs would be reduced now that £40 per day is offered as bonus. With normal costs £1,130 this would be reduced by (5 x £40) - (£5 x £20) = £100, giving £1,030 overall cost for a total project time of 33 - 5 = 28 days. As in the previous example, activity B and activity E would be considered together to save 1 day on the overall project time. The total cost for both activities is £50 per day and with a bonus being given of £40 per day it is not worth considering. The same applies to activity H where the costs are £45 per day which, compared with the £40 bonus, is also not worth further consideration.

The optimum plan would be to have the overall time at 28 days, costing £1,030.

When a network plan is complete, including any resource allocation or cost evaluation that may have been necessary, the work is scheduled and progress control starts.

To be effective a plan must be dynamic. Means must exist for following changing circumstances and evaluating quickly the information needed for central decisions to be made. Networks can provide central information readily if they are regularly brought up to date as the project proceeds. If a delay occurs, say in the delivery of plant or materials, its effect on the project can be seen quickly. The critical path may change. Examination of what must be done on the critical path to make up lost time by perhaps rearranging the project or accelerating some of the activities on the critical path needs to be made. The tendency disappears to 'crash' everything when a project gets behind schedule.

Updating the network at agreed intervals is of vital importance if the full value of network planning is to be realised. Analysing the network without the use of a computer is possible up to about 150 activities, beyond this the sheer amount of arithmetical calculations with updating, warrants the use of computer packages.

Network planning is a management tool of great impact which makes possible more effective discharge of a project. Its main attraction lies in the simplicity of the basic concept which enables all concerned to participate in its use. Its power lies in the discipline it provides and its future promise of significant advance in the treatment of time/cost/resource relationships.

It is by no means confined to civil engineering projects, as already it has made great impact on marketing and development. It is being used also in research, commercial and general management fields. Networks are likely to prove of value in any project which has many interdependent activities and has to be completed within stipulated time or cost limits.

EXERCISES

1. (a) Explain with the help of two examples the principal uses of
dummies in constructing networks.

   (b) Draw the network for the following project. Calculate the
earliest and latest times at the events and identify the
critical path.

   (c) Explain briefly how to calculate the earliest and latest
times at the events, when several activities meet at an event.

Activity	Duration	Preceded by
A	2	-
B	1	-
C	3	-
D	2	A
E	4	A
F	8	C
G	2	C
H	5	D and F and G
J	4	E and F and G
K	2	B and F and G
L	6	M and J and K

2. A network for a project is presented below. The duration time
for the activities are normal times in days.

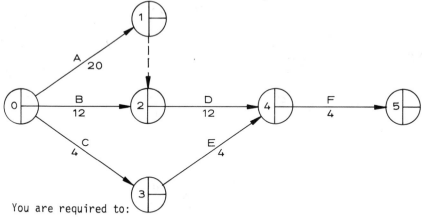

You are required to:

(a) Calculate the earliest starting time and the latest starting

75

time for each activity.

(b) Determine the critical path.

(c) Calculate the total cost for the project if each separate normal activity uses resources which cost £100 per week and there is an additional indirect cost of £200 for every week the project is in progress.

(d) What is the optimum cost plan for the project if each activity can be progressively reduced by one week at an extra cost as follows:

Activity	Cost per week saved (£)
A	100
B	90
C	75
D	150
E	250
F	400

3. A project consists of the following activities:

A and B can be performed in parallel.
A must be performed before C, D and E which are independent of each other.
F cannot start until D is finished.
G cannot start until C and D are finished.
F must be finished before H and I can start.
E and I must be finished before J can start.
G and H must be finished before K can start.
L cannot start until J and K are complete.
The project is complete when L and B have been completed.

The duration in days of each activity is as follows:

A	6	B	32
C	5	D	7
E	12	F	5
G	10	H	6
I	5	J	4
K	9	L	7

You are required to:

(a) Draw the network and define the critical path.

(b) Construct a schedule showing the earliest and latest start times, the earliest and latest finish times of each activity, together with the independent float.

76

SOLUTIONS TO EXERCISES

1. (a)

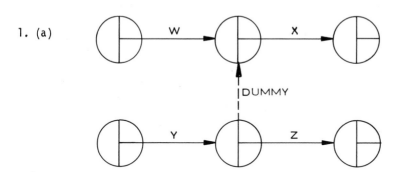

To assist in the logic of the network, activities are where time and resources are used. In the example X depends on W and Y but is independent of Z. Activity Z depends only on Y.

To avoid two activities having the same numbers at the head and tail, which would cause confusion:

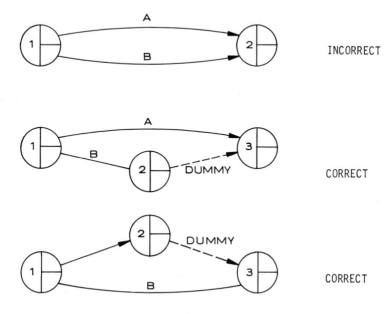

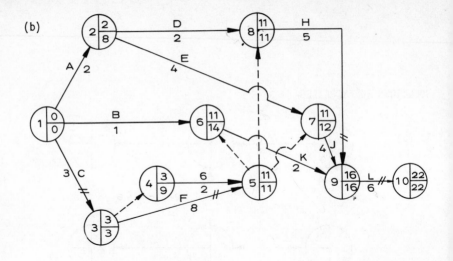

Critical Path 1 - 3 - 5 - 8 - 9 - 10

(c) Earliest event time

When several activities meet at an event, the earliest event time is the largest of times entering the event.

Latest event time

The easiest way to calculate this is to work backwards through the network from the final event and at each event check what is the latest time you can leave the event being considered, without affecting the calculated overall project time.

2. (a)

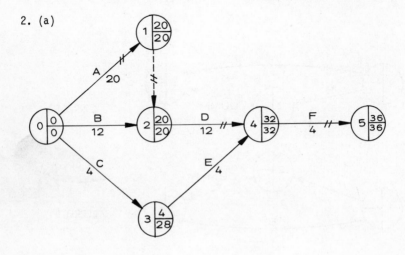

Activity	Earliest start	Latest start
A	0	0
B	0	8
C	0	24
D	20	20
E	4	28
F	32	32

(b) Critical Path 0 - 1 - 2 - 4 - 5

(c) Total cost 36 weeks x £200 indirect costs = £7,200
20 weeks x £100 = £2,000
12 weeks x £100 = £1,200
12 weeks x £100 = £1,200
4 weeks x £100 = £ 400
4 weeks x £100 = £ 400
4 weeks x £100 = £ 400

Total =£12,800

(d)
Reduce	by	cost	saving	balance	project duration
A	8 weeks	8 x 100	8 x 200	£800	28 weeks
D	11 weeks	11 x 150	11 x 200	£550	17 weeks
A and B	5 weeks	5 x 190	5 x 200	£ 50	12 weeks
			Total	£1,400	

Optimum cost plan: 12 days costing £12,800 - £1400 = £11,400.

3. (a)

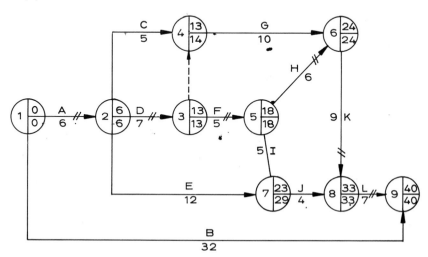

3. (b) Schedule:

Activity	Duration	Start Earliest	Start Latest	Finish Earliest	Finish Latest	Independent Float
A	6	0	0	6	6	0
B	32	0	8	32	40	8
C	5	6	9	11	14	3
D	7	6	6	13	13	0
E	12	6	17	18	29	11
F	5	13,	13	18	18	0
G	10	13	14	23	24	1
H	6	18	18	24	24	0
I	5	18	24	23	29	6
J	4	23	29	27	33	6
K	9	24	24	33	33	0
L	7	33	33	40	40	0

Applications

1. BUILDING CONSTRUCTION LIMITED

A report had been issued by the construction department of Building Construction Limited to the network analyst employed by the company giving complete details of the procedure for the future construction of a distillation column.

The complaint from the network analyst was that instead of issuing a written report on the procedure to be adopted for construction, together with time scales and costs, it would have been better presented in the form of a schedule or list.

The report issued read as follows.

Report Number 7

Construction of a distillation column

Before any 'mechanical design of ends and shells' is undertaken by the company a 'plant definition' must be obtained for which four days should be allowed at a normal cost of £1,000. Immediately afterwards the design can be carried out in three days for £1,000. The extra cost for the saving of one day on this activity is £250. Two days could be saved if necessary.

The 'issue of schedules for ends and shells' follows 'mechanical design' duration two days, normal cost £1,000 although one day could be saved for £250 cost.

'Requisition ends and shells' is next, followed by 'order ends and shells', both taking one day for £100 normal cost each.

The activity causing the greatest amount of time is 'procure ends and shells' which takes twenty-four days at normal cost of £3,000 although five days could be saved if required at £150 per day.

After 'mechanical design of ends and shells' it would be also possible to have activity 'mechanical design of the remainder of upper column' completed in six days at £1,000 cost but three days could be saved at £50 per day.

'Issue schedules for remainder of upper column' would follow, duration two days at £1,000 cost.

81

'Material planning' is next in two days, costing £300 with one day possible for reduction in time at £40.

'Work layouts' immediately follow with four days' duration allowed but two days could be saved at £30 per day. Normal cost £600. Follow with 'documentation' which should be completed in one day at £150.

After 'procure ends and shells' and 'documentation' the next activity will be 'roll shells and weld ends' for which three days is allocated at £450.

Returning to 'material planning', after this activity 'test' could be carried out in one day at £150, followed by 'order materials' in one day at £100. Sixteen days will be required for the next activity 'procure materials' costing £5,000 although five days could be saved at £100 per day.

The activity to follow both 'procure materials' and 'roll shells and weld ends' will be 'complete fabrication and assembly of upper column' allowing five days at the cost of £750 with the saving of two days possible at £350 per day.

The last three activities in order will be 'test', 'pack' and 'despatch', each taking one day at £150 cost.

The network analyst considered it highly desirable to extract the necessary information and data and list under the headings:

Activity
Description
Preceding activity
Duration (days)
Normal cost
Extra cost of saving one day
Days that could be saved.

From this list produce the network and,

(a) state the activities on the critical path;
(b) calculate the time to complete at the normal cost;
(c) calculate the cost of completing in 40 days, indicating the activities that would be reduced.

Discussion

Discuss the effect of failure to complete activities 'procure ends and shells' and 'procure materials' in the estimated duration. State the advice you would offer to the management if there were two alternative suppliers of the materials involved in activity 'procure materials':

Supplier X, for delivery in 10 days quoted £5,000 $\pm$ £100 for every day early or late.
Supplier Y, for delivery in 19 days, quoted £4,000 $\pm$ £500 for every day early or late.

The following activities are necessary to construct a distillation column

Activity	Description	Preceding Activity	Duration (days)	Normal Cost (£)	Extra cost of saving one day (£)	Days that could be saved
A	Plant definition	-	4	1,000	-	-
B	Mechanical design of ends and shells	A	3	1,000	250	2
C	Issue schedules for ends and shells	B	2	1,000	250	1
D	Requisition ends and shells	C	1	100	-	-
E	Order ends and shells	D	1	100	-	-
F	Procure ends and shells	E	24	3,000	150	5
G	Roll shells and weld ends	F, T	3	450	-	-
H	Complete fabrication and assembly of upper column	G, R	5	750	350	2
I	Test	H	1	150	-	-
J	Pack	I	1	150	-	-
K	Despatch	J	1	150	-	-
L	Mechanical design of remainder of upper column	B	6	1,000	50	3
M	Issue schedules for remainder of upper column	L	2	1,000	-	-
N	Material planning	M	2	300	40	1
P	Requisition materials	N	1	100	-	-
Q	Order materials	P	1	100	-	-
R	Procure materials	Q	16	5,000	100	5
S	Work layouts	N	4	600	30	2
T	Documentation	S	1	150	-	-
			Total	£16,100		

2. CLEANABUILD LIMITED

Cleanabuild were specialists in cleaning the exterior walls of old buildings in the hearts of big cities. They obtained a prestige contract for cleaning 17 buildings of historic interest in a famous London street.

The basic requirements for such a contract are labour and equipment. The labour force can be considered to be a specific number of men as, due to the nature of the work, all the men employed can be used on any job involved in the cleaning process. The equipment to be used consists of units of plant, each with a compressor and a water pump, feeding a number of handheld units. The limitations on the distance of handheld units from the compressor and pump are taken into consideration before bidding for the work.

This particular contract, whilst giving the company the maximum of publicity was nevertheless a comparatively straightforward series of cleaning jobs that warranted no special approach, except to complete them by the specified time and make a profit. There was, however, a series of constraints laid down by the organisation letting out the work. The buildings were numbered 1 - 17 respectively and the constraints were:-

(1) The whole contract was to be completed in 26 weeks.

(2) Certain localised priorities and discussions with the local police regarding traffic problems, together with insurance factors, led to certain priorities of cleaning and these were:

    (a) Buildings numbers 1 and 3 must be cleaned at the same time but number 4 cannot be started until they are completed.

    (b) Buildings numbers 7, 9, 11, 13 and 15 must be cleaned in that order.

    (c) Buildings numbers 4, 6 and 8 must be cleaned in that order.

    (d) Number 14 must be cleaned after number 16 has been finished and before number 7 is started.

    (e) Number 12 must follow number 10 and number 13 must follow number 11, but both the two pairs must be cleaned during the same period.

    (f) The whole contract must commence with number 2 and then followed by numbers 3, 16 and 17, all starting on the completion of number 2. Number 1 can be started as soon as number 17 is finished.

    (g) Number 5 cannot be started before number 3 is completed and number 7 cannot be started until number 5 is finished.

    (h) Number 8 must be completed before number 11 can be started.

A schedule showing the amount of labour necessary for each building, the amount of plant required and the time in weeks to complete the buildings was prepared by the Contract Manager. The complete schedule is as follows:

Schedule 1

Building number	Number of men	Number of Plant units	Time in weeks
1	3	2	4
2	4	4	6
3	3	1	2
4	2	2	2
5	4	4	7
6	3	4	6
7	2	2	1
8	3	2	2
9	3	3	1
10	4	1	3
11	2	3	2
12	3	3	4
13	2	1	1
14	4	3	4
15	3	2	2
16	2	2	1
17	4	1	3

Costs

The overheads on the whole contract were calculated to be £330 per week. Labour costs were to be £120 per man per week and plant £200 per unit per week.

From the schedule it was obvious that it would not be possible to complete the contract in the specified time. Accordingly, the Contract Manager prepared a second schedule which showed the requirements of labour and plant to reduce the activity times and details of the time that could be saved.

The second schedule was as follows:

Schedule 2

Building number	Number of men extra	Number of Plant units extra	Savings in weeks on contract time
1	2	1	1
2	2	2	2
3	0	0	0
4	0	0	0
5	2	0	1
6	1	0	1

Building number	Number of men extra	Number of plant units extra	Savings in weeks on contract time
7	0	0	0
8	0	1	1
9	0	0	0
10	0	2	1
11	1	0	1
12	2	2	2
13	0	0	0
14	1	1	1
15	2	0	1
16	0	0	0
17	0	2	1

The Contracts Manager based on these two schedules an overall plan for the contract and presented it to the planning committee. The Managing Director agreed in principle with the plan put forward, however, he pointed out that this was THE prestige contract and that any contract could be completed in a shorter time than originally planned and at a lower cost. He stressed that the company could not under any circumstances afford any adverse publicity of late completion and so any possibility of finishing before the specified date would give them extra insurance. He then asked the committee to produce a new contract plan based on the following specifications:

(1) To plan to complete the contract in the minimum time for maximum profit.

(2) To prepare a work schedule for the buildings that would utilise the labour and plant to maximum efficiency.

(3) To prepare a resource schedule that would show the usage of labour and plant throughout the contract.

How should the committee proceed to meet this specification and what final solution would it produce?

Discussion

The Managing Director, on receiving the schedule for the 23 week project time, stated that he would approve a 22 week overall completion time, which no doubt would reduce the present estimated cost of £54,390. Is this possible under present conditions?

Solutions to applications

1. Building Construction Limited

Network 1.

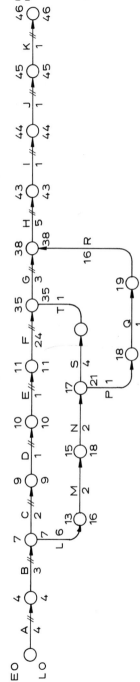

The critical activities are A-B-C-D-E-F-G-H-I-J-K

The time to complete at normal cost = 46 days

Normal cost = £16,100.

There is no point in reducing activities S at £30, N at £40, L at £50 and R at £100 per day because these activities are not on the critical path. Any reduction of these activities would not at this stage reduce the overall project time.

Consider activity F, which at £150 per day is a critical activity and it is possible to reduce this by 3 days. The network would be as Network 2. Costs now would be £16,100 + (3 × £150) = £16,550.

Network 2.

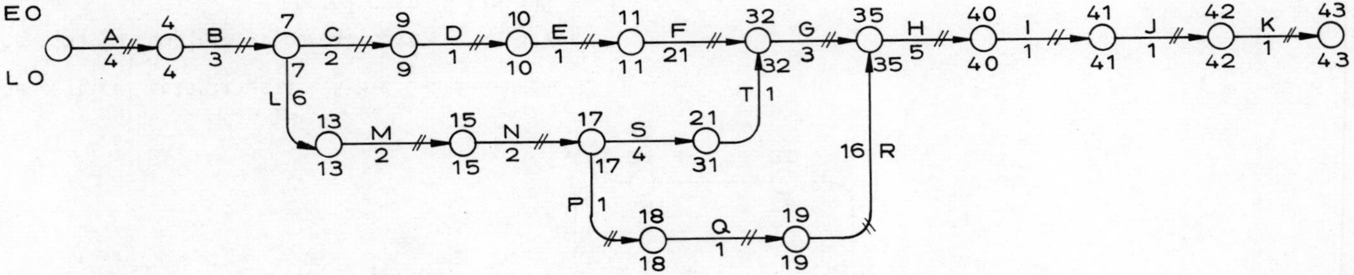

EO

LO

A 4
4

B 3
4

C 2
7
7

L 6

D 1
9
9

E 1
10
10

F 21
11
11

G 3
32
32

H 5
35
35

I 1
40
40

J 1
41
41

K 1
42
42

43
43

M 2
13
13

N 2
15
15

S 4
17
17

T 1
21
31

P 1
18
18

Q 1
19
19

R 16

A second critical path is formed A-B-L-M-N-P-Q-R-H-I-J-K of duration 43 days. Cost £16,550.

Reduce activity B by 2 days at £250 per day = £500. Network 3 is formed with costs now £16,550 + £500 = £17,050.

88

Network 3.

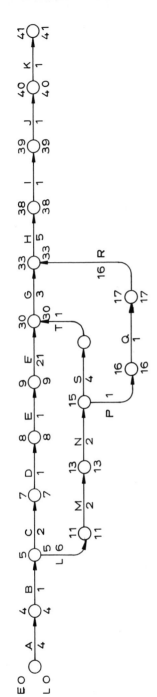

The critical path remains as Network 2. Duration 41 days at a cost of £17,050.

We are required to reduce by 1 further day to achieve 40 days total project time. Reduce activity H by 1 day at £350, which forms Network 4. Total cost £17,050 + £350 = £17,400.

89

Network 4.

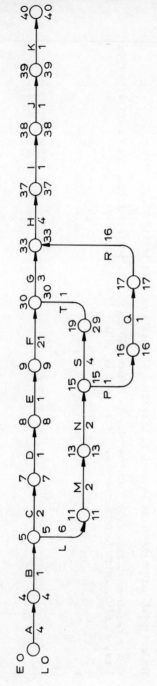

The final network contains two critical paths: A-B-C-D-E-F-G-H-I-J-K and A-B-L-M-N-P-Q-R-H-I-J-K. The activities that have been reduced are F, B and H. Duration 40 days at a cost of £17,400.

If activities F and R are not completed on time a delay will occur as both these activities are on the critical path.

90

2. Cleanabuild Limited

Resource Requirements:

		Cost (£)
Labour (Men) x £120 (cost) x 169 (man weeks)		20,280
Plant (Plant) x £200 (cost) x 142 (plant weeks)		28,400
Overheads £330 (cost) x 32 (weeks)		10,560
	Figure 1. Total cost	£59,240

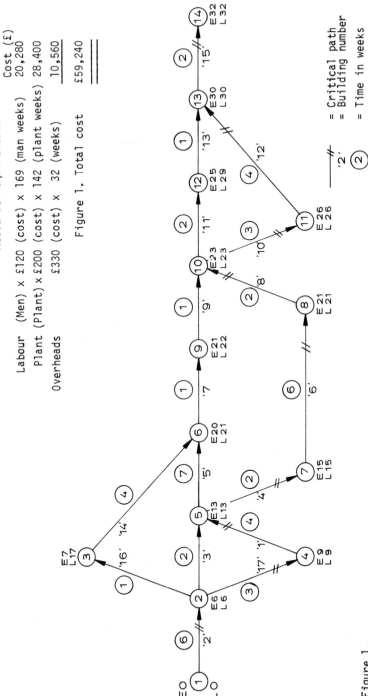

Figure 1.

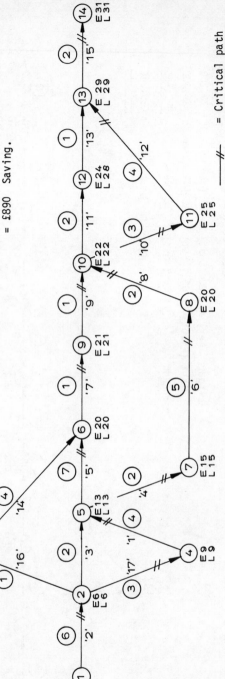

Cleanabuild Limited

Resource Requirements:

		Cost (£)
Labour (Men) x £120 (cost) x 171 (man weeks)		20,520
Plant (Plant) x £200 (cost) x 138 (plant weeks)		27,600
Overheads £330 (cost) x 31 (weeks)		10,230
	Figure 2. Total cost	£58,350

Total cost (Figure 1) £59,240 – Total cost (Fig.2) £58,350

= £890 Saving.

∕∕ = Critical path

'2' = Time in weeks

② = Building number

Figure 2.   Reducing Building 6 by 1 Week – From 6 to 5 Weeks

92

Cleanabuild Limited

Resource Requirements:

				Cost (£)
Labour	(Men)	x £120 (cost)	x 176 (man weeks)	21,120
Plant	(Plant)	x £200 (cost)	x 133 (plant weeks)	26,600
Overheads		£330 (cost)	x 30 (weeks)	9,900

Figure 3. Total cost   £57,620

Total cost (Fig.2) £58,350 — Total cost (Fig.3) £57,620

= £730 Saving.

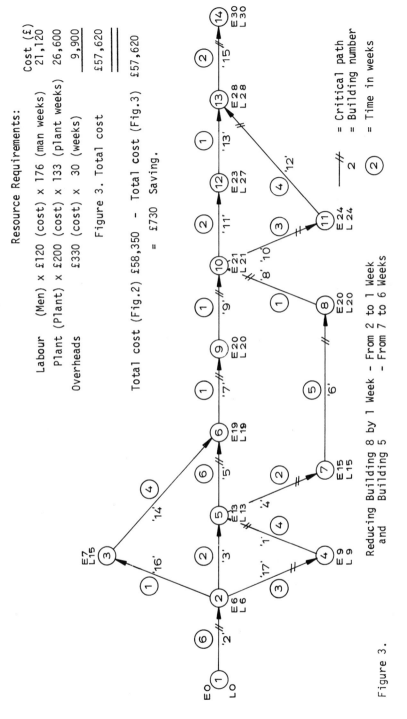

Reducing Building 8 by 1 Week - From 2 to 1 Week
        and   Building 5   - From 7 to 6 Weeks

Figure 3.

—//— = Critical path
2 = Building number
② = Time in weeks

93

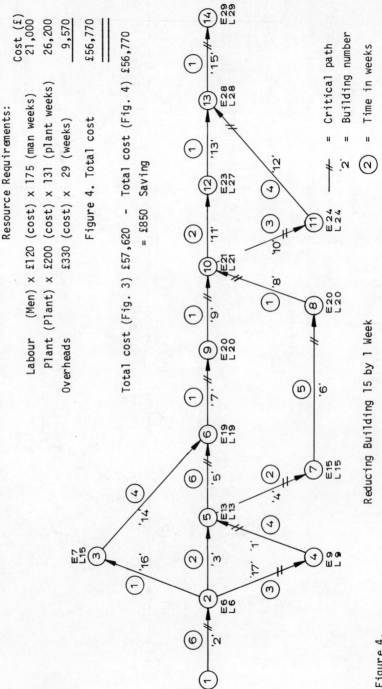

Cleanabuild Limited

Resource Requirements:

		Cost (£)
Labour (Men) x £120 (cost) x 175 (man weeks)		21,000
Plant (Plant) x £200 (cost) x 131 (plant weeks)		26,200
Overheads £330 (cost) x 29 (weeks)		9,570
		£56,770

Figure 4. Total cost

Total cost (Fig. 3) £57,620 − Total cost (Fig. 4) £56,770
= £850   Saving

Reducing Building 15 by 1 Week

—//— = Critical path

'2' = Time in weeks

(2) = Building number

Figure 4.

Cleanabuild Limited

Resource Requirements:

			Cost (£)
Labour	(Men)	x £120 (cost) x 173 (man weeks)	20,760
Plant	(Plant)	x £200 (cost) x 129 (plant weeks)	25,800
Overheads		£330 (cost) x 27 (weeks)	8,910

Figure 5. Total cost   £55,470

Total cost (Fig. 4) £56,770 – Total cost (Fig. 5) £55,470
= £1,300 Saving

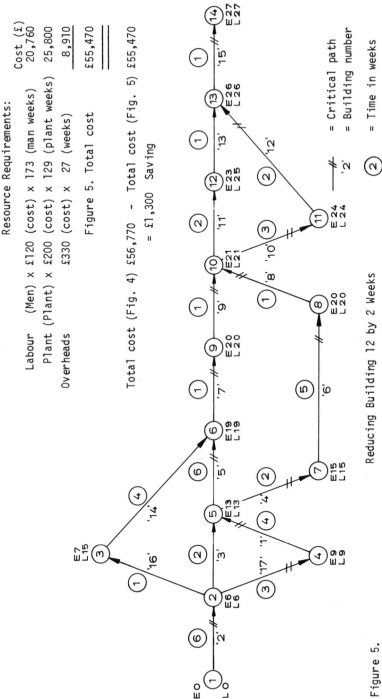

Reducing Building 12 by 2 Weeks

Figure 5.

95

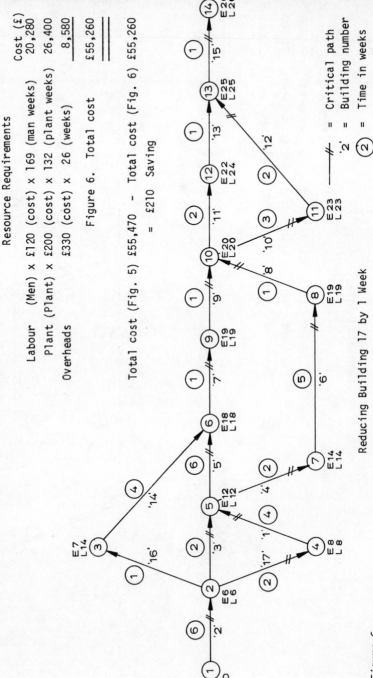

Cleanabuild Limited

Resource Requirements

		Cost (£)
Labour (Men) x £120 (cost) x 169 (man weeks)		20,280
Plant (Plant) x £200 (cost) x 132 (plant weeks)		26,400
Overheads £330 (cost) x 26 (weeks)		8,580
		£55,260

Figure 6. Total cost

Total cost (Fig. 5) £55,470 - Total cost (Fig. 6) £55,260

= £210 Saving

Reducing Building 17 by 1 Week

—————— = Critical path

'2' = Building number

② = Time in weeks

Figure 6.

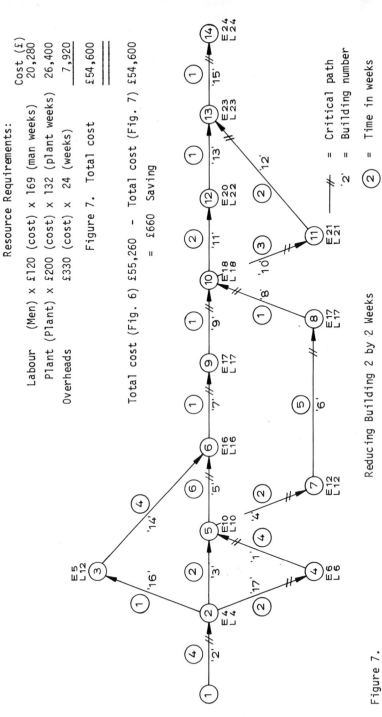

Cleanabuild Limited

Resource Requirements:

				Cost (£)
Labour	(Men) x £120 (cost) x 169 (man weeks)			20,280
Plant	(Plant) x £200 (cost) x 132 (plant weeks)			26,400
Overheads	£330 (cost) x 24 (weeks)			7,920

Figure 7. Total cost £54,600

Total cost (Fig. 6) £55,260 - Total cost (Fig. 7) £54,600

= £660 Saving

Reducing Building 2 by 2 Weeks

———— = Critical path

'2' = Building number

② = Time in weeks

Figure 7.

97

Cleanabuild Limited

Resource Requirements:

			Cost (£)
Labour (Men)	x £120 (cost)	x 165 (man weeks)	19,800
Plant (Plant)	x £200 (cost)	x 135 (plant weeks)	27,000
Overheads	£330 (cost)	x 23 (weeks)	7,590
		Total cost	£54,390

Figure 8. Total cost

Total cost (Fig. 7) £54,600 - Total cost (Fig. 8) £54,390
                              = £210 Saving.

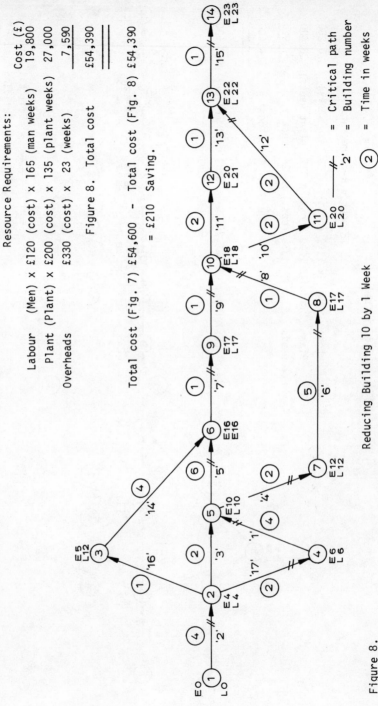

Reducing Building 10 by 1 Week

——— = Critical path

'2' = Building number

② = Time in weeks

Figure 8.

98

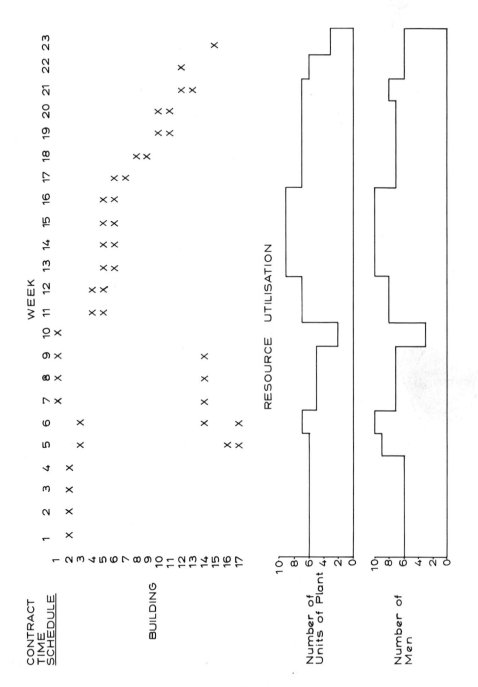

CLEANABUILD LIMITED

CONCLUSION

By logical analysis of the contract constraints the network shown in
Figure 1 can be developed.

The critical path is 1-2-4-5-7-8-10-11-13-14 with a total time of
32 weeks and a total cost of £59,240. This comprises of 169 man-weeks
(£20,280), 142 plant-weeks (£28,400) and overheads of 32 weeks
(£10,560).

Using the costing information the following analysis is possible.

Number of weeks for completion		Building number to be completed to give reduced cost	Total cost
32	Figure 1		£59,240
31	Figure 2	6-	£58,350
30	Figure 3	6-8-5	£57,620
29	Figure 4	6-8-5-15	£56,770
27	Figure 5	6-8-5-15-12	£55,470
26	Figure 6	6-8-5-15-12-17	£55,260
24	Figure 7	6-8-5-15-12-17-2	£54,600
23	Figure 8	6-8-5-15-12-17-2-10	£54,390

For the 23 week schedule the cost comprises of 165 man-weeks (£19,800),
135 plant-weeks (£27,000) with overheads of 23 weeks (£7,590),
totalling £54,390.

The critical paths being

    1-2-4-5-7-8-10-11-13-14 and

    1-2-4-5-6-9-10-11-13-14.

5 Simulation

There are two methods of solving a problem:

1. Reduce the problem to an equation, set of equations or set of inequalities, solve the problem, and by doing so this is called the analytical approach.

2. To carry out a set or series of tests and then by trial and error to select a solution, in this case it would be called the heuristic approach.

A good example of the analytical approach is, that by manipulating the models in linear programming we arrive at an optimal solution, usually minimising costs or maximising profit which becomes a unique solution to the problem. In the heuristic approach a series of alternative solutions to the problem are available which may not include the optimal one.

In many cases a 'good solution' would be acceptable rather than the optimum one, because of the time and cost necessary to obtain it. Many models can be complex mathematically and not all problems can be stated in mathematical terms. For this reason simulation can be invaluable.

In simulation one is endeavouring to construct <u>a model of the real</u> <u>situation</u> and by manipulating the model, usually on a computer, a series of solutions become available for choice.

Monte Carlo simulation

Monte Carlo is a heuristic technique which generates frequency distributions. We can take an example of a car which in a very modern garage must attend and take its place in three queues. The first queue is to have the underside of the car inspected, the second for external body rust and the third to look at the report and obtain an appointment. The average or mean time each car spends in each queue is:

Queue	Minutes
1	15
2	25
3	10
Total	50

The danger of the 'overworked average' can be misleading here, that all cars are away from the garage in 50 minutes is far from true, as can be seen from the frequency distribution of 100 cars. The mean time for carrying out the three tasks in the garage is approximately

50 minutes, but nine cars in fact are in the garage 70 minutes or more and one, no doubt fuming, driver for 80 minutes plus.

Table 5.1.

Frequency distribution times of 100 cars

Minutes	Frequency of cars	Cumulative frequency
30 - 34	3	3
35 - 39	13	16
40 - 44	24	40
45 - 49	18	58
50 - 54	14	72
55 - 59	10	82
60 - 64	6	88
65 - 69	3	91
70 - 74	5	96
75 - 79	3	99
80 - 84	1	100
	Total 100	

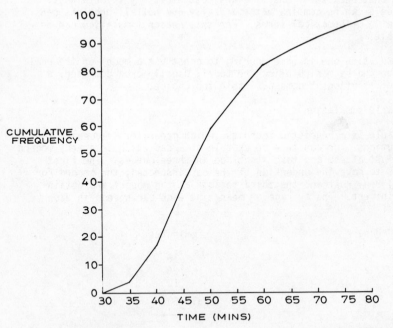

Figure 5.1. A cumulative frequency distribution for the waiting time of 100 cars.

102

To stress the danger of an 'average', a man who was a non-swimmer was told that there should be no problem wading across a calm stretch of water because the average depth was two feet. He noticed how shallow it was at the edge and waded into the water. Unfortunately he was not told the depth in the middle was ten feet, he drowned!!

If the outcome of the system can be represented by drawing random samples from a series of frequency distributions, we can use the Monte Carlo method to simulate the system. One of the great advantages of the Monte Carlo method is when the data forming the distribution is not of a standard type of distribution or irregular shaped.

Monte Carlo simulation is used for solving queueing type problems. The method assumes that:

(a) one can represent a system as a series of component parts, and

(b) one can predict the probability of a component part being in any one of a finite number of possible states at any given time.

Sampling from a series of frequencies enables the system to be simulated.

If we consider an assembly line where the flow of work is set so that parts arrive at equal intervals of time, we do not have problems of queueing. It is the time gaps between arrivals dispersed around the mean time which causes waiting time. An example using the Monte Carlo method can be applied to the following problem.

EXAMPLE 1

Workers in a factory arrive at random intervals of time to a tool stores which has a single serving hatch. The workers are serviced by the storekeeper to their requirements, and the servicing times are also random. By observing and recording times with a stop watch the two frequency distributions were obtained covering 100 arrivals and servicing times. For times between arrivals the frequency distribution was:

Table 5.2.

Time between arrivals and percentage frequency
of occurrence

Time gap (min.)	Frequency of occurrence (%)	Random numbers allocated to class
6	10	0 - 9
7	15	10 - 24
8	25	25 - 49
9	35	50 - 84
10	15	85 - 99
	Total 100	

103

Random numbers have been allocated proportionately to the frequency of occurrence in each class. The 6 minute time interval which has a frequency of 10 has been allocated random numbers 0-9 inclusive. Time interval 7 with frequency 15, has 10-24 inclusive random numbers allocated to it and so on until the total frequencies are catered for. The time for servicing forms the second frequency distribution.

Table 5.3.
Service times and percentage frequency of occurrence

Service time (min.)	Frequency of occurrence (%)	Random numbers allocated to class
7	5	0 - 4
8	15	5 - 19
9	20	20 - 39
10	25	40 - 64
11	15	65 - 79
12	20	80 - 99
Total	100	

The simulation will consist of the arrival of a worker to the stores which we will call time zero, to get the simulation started. The storekeeper at this stage will be available for service, the time to service will be obtained by sampling from the frequency distribution using random numbers. The time gap for the next worker will be obtained in the same way, but from the frequency distribution of times between arrivals. By continually sampling from both distributions in sequence, we can find the time the workers are waiting for service and thus the average waiting time also for the storekeeper.

Throughout the simulation assume a clock is continually running and at the start the worker in the system is at 0, waiting to be served. The storekeeper is available also at 0 therefore neither have to wait. To find the service time we look up the random number tables and in this example twenty numbers are listed, 62, 27, 69, 02, 51, 6, 90, 17, 41, 14, 20, 74, 94, 22, 93, 45, 44, 16, 04 and 32. The first number 62 represents a service time of 10 minutes obtained from the frequency distribution Table 5.3. Random number 27 gives 9 minutes, and random number 69, 11 minutes and so on. To obtain times between arrivals twenty random numbers are listed and the same procedure is adopted, this time sampling from Table 5.2.

From the simulation it can be seen that the first service is completed at 10 minutes and the second worker also arrives at 10, therefore no waiting is required. With a service time of 9 minutes for worker number two, his departure time will be at 10 + 9 = 19 minutes. Arrival time for worker three is at 10 + 8 = 18 minutes, thus the worker will wait from 18 to 19 = 1 minute, which is recorded under waiting time for the third worker and so on through the simulation.

Table 5.4.
A typical simulation of waiting time for worker and storekeeper for Example 1

Worker	Random number	Time between arrivals (min.)	Cumulative arrival time	Random number	Service time	Time serviced	Cumulative departure time	Waiting Time Worker	Waiting Time Stores
1	-	-	0	62	10	0	10	0	0
2	95	10	10	27	9	10	19	0	0
3	48	8	18	69	11	19	30	1	0
4	10	7	25	02	7	30	37	5	0
5	88	10	35	51	10	37	47	2	0
6	07	6	41	06	8	47	55	6	0
7	15	7	48	90	12	55	67	7	0
8	26	8	56	17	8	67	75	11	0
9	42	8	64	41	10	75	85	11	0
10	05	6	70	14	8	85	93	15	0
11	03	6	76	20	9	93	101	17	0
12	62	9	85	74	11	101	112	16	0
13	61	9	94	94	12	112	124	18	0
14	89	10	104	22	9	124	133	20	0
15	01	6	110	93	12	133	145	23	0
16	27	8	118	45	10	145	155	27	0
17	49	8	126	44	10	155	165	29	0
18	20	7	133	16	8	165	173	32	0
19	48	8	141	04	7	173	180	32	0
20	08	6	147	32	9	180	189	33	0

In this example the average time for waiting by a worker is

$$\frac{305}{20} = 15.2 \text{ minutes}$$

We can see the danger of taking an average figure, even in this simple example most of the workers will wait longer than this, when waiting. With the present system there is little chance of waiting time decreasing, in fact the reverse. A longer simulation would show this. The storekeeper would rarely wait for someone to serve, in fact he would be an extremely busy individual.

With the Monte Carlo method we are simulating a system and not sampling from a population, therefore we can place confidence levels on the results obtained from the simulation. We can, however, run the simulation long enough on a computer to obtain stability which is when the results oscillate within the boundaries of a predetermined error rate.

In our example of the workers and stores, even if the mean time of arrival and servicing time had been identical, it would not be possible to say that there would be no queueing time or idle time for the storekeeper. It is worth repeating that these factors depend on the dispersion of the actual times around the mean time and the wider the dispersion the greater the waiting or idle time.

Having obtained that waiting or idle time exists we may not be happy with the present system, for instance assume the waiting time for workers over 10 minutes is not acceptable. Three possibilities can be considered:

1. Regulate the flow of arrivals which would reduce the dispersion.

2. Reduce the volume of arrivals.

3. Increase the service facility, e.g. extra servicing hatch and
   storekeeper.

Assuming that 1 and 2 are not feasible, which is often the situation, we are faced with the cost of providing the extra servicing facility. We need to compare the extra cost of the service against the decreasing cost of waiting time.

In our example the company needs to decide whether to increase the service facility, if so by how many? The building extension costs spread over many thousands of hours is negligible. The running costs for one hatch is £25 per hour and it is estimated that each additional hatch would increase by £20 per hour. The value of a skilled worker to the company is £60 per hour and the waiting time shows an average of 15 minutes approximately for each worker. This would be the cost with only one hatch being available, as at present, of £15. Assuming that with two hatches, waiting time by the worker is removed or negligible (the student can simulate for two and three hatches as an exercise and perhaps confirm this) costs for waiting will be zero. The following table can be drawn up and costs presented.

(1) Number of hatches (x)	(2) Total hourly cost of (x) hatches (£)	(3) Average cost of workers' waiting time (£)	(4) (2) + (3) (£)
1	25	15	40
2	45	0	45
3	65	0	65

Based only on costs, it would not pay the company to extend the stores facilities.

If we review our simulation carefully it is obvious that the workers' waiting time is steadily increasing and by worker number 20 his waiting time is 33 minutes. The danger of an average has been stressed, also we can see the results of conclusions from a small simulation. If we take the waiting time of workers being in the region of 30 minutes and recalculate for the extension of the stores we would obtain the following:

(1) Number of hatches (x)	(2) Total hourly cost of (x) hatches (£)	(3) Average cost of workers' waiting time (£)	(4) (2) + (3) (£)
1	25	30	55
2	45	0	45
3	65	0	65

We would now recommend that, based on costs, there should be an extra hatch installed with service facilities as soon as possible.

There are three advantages in using simulation:

1. By altering a single parameter in the system the results or likely results of the change can be calculated. Thus many alternatives can be tested.

2. The results of changes in 1 can be obtained quickly rather than over a period of perhaps years by the real life system.

3. Resulting from 1 and 2 enormous costs could be saved.

Little mention has been made of the computer, but its sheer presence has expedited the use of simulation because of its speed of calculation and storage capacity. The computer can generate its own random numbers and the complexity of the simulation is only limited by the size of the fast access store.

EXERCISES

1. A large store purchases crates of eggs from a local dairy produce marketing board daily. The average cost to the stores of an individual crate is £5 and the average return per crate after sale to the public is £7 if the eggs are sold the same day. At the end of each day it is the stores policy to dispose of the crates to the staff at £2 per crate.

   Records of purchases and customer demand over 250 working days are:

Number of crates purchased	Number of days	Number of crates demanded	Number of days
14	30	14	40
15	50	15	50
16	70	16	70
17	70	17	60
18	30	18	30
	250		250

   Using the table of random numbers, simulate the purchase and demand over the next ten days, showing the daily and cumulative profit.

2. A factory employs three breakdown crews to repair machines which fail. Whenever a breakdown occurs one complete crew only attend and when the failure does occur one complete day can be safely assumed to rectify the machine. This information being available from past data. The following frequency table indicates the distribution of machine breakdowns per day. Use Monte Carlo methods to determine the adequacy or otherwise of the maintenance system at present in operation at the factory. Simulate for 20 days.

   Machine breakdowns per day:

Number of breakdowns	Number of days
0	8
1	15
2	15
3	30
4	20
5	7
6	5
Total	100

3. A sample of 100 arrivals of customers at a cash desk in a
   supermarket is according to the following data:

Time between arrivals in minutes	Frequency
0.5	2
1.0	6
1.5	10
2.0	25
2.5	20
3.0	14
3.5	10
4.0	7
4.5	4
5.0	2
	100

Observation of the time to service each customer by totalling up
the receiving payment, giving change and placing goods aside for
packing, etc. gives the following data:

Service time in minutes	Frequency
0.5	15
1.0	18
1.5	38
2.0	16
2.5	7
3.0	6
	100

Using the random number tables, Monte Carlo simulate a sample of
15 customers and calculate the average per cent customer waiting
time and the average per cent cashier idle time.

SOLUTIONS TO EXERCISES

1. Purchases:

Purchase	Number of days	% Probabilities	Cumulative Probabilities	Random Number
14	30	12	12	0 - 11
15	50	20	32	12 - 31
16	70	28	60	32 - 59
17	70	28	88	60 - 87
18	30	12	100	88 - 99
		100		

Demand:

Demand	Number of days	% Probabilities	Cumulative Probabilities	Random Number
14	40	16	16	0 - 15
15·	50	20	36	16 - 35
16	70	28	64	36 - 63
17	60	24	88	64 - 87
18	30	12	100	88 - 99
		100		

Typical simulation:

Day	R.N.	Units Bought	Cost	R.N.	Units Demanded	Income	Daily Profit (+ or -)	Cumulative Profit
1	25	15	75	42	16	105	+ 30	30
2	52	16	80	23	15	107	+ 27	57
3	55	16	80	59	16	112	+ 22	79
4	10	14	70	38	16	98	+ 28	107
5	61	17	85	02	14	104	+ 19	116
6	66	17	85	86	17	119	+ 34	150
7	17	15	75	51	16	105	+ 30	180
8	28	15	75	92	18	105	+ 30	210
9	17	15	75	44	16	105	+ 30	240
10	20	15	75	19	15	105	+ 30	270

2. Allocating random numbers to the frequency of days breakdowns
   occur the following table is obtained:

Number of breakdowns	Number of days	%	%	R.N.
0	8	8	8	0 - 7
1	15	15	23	8 - 22
2	15	15	38	23 - 37
3	30	30	68	38 - 67
4	20	20	88	68 - 87
5	7	7	95	88 - 94
6	5	5	100	95 - 99
	Total 100			

Typical 20 day simulation:

Day	R.N.	Number of breakdowns	Number of crews used	Machines not repaired	Crews not used
1	14	1	1	0	2
2	32	2	2	0	1
3	07	0	0	0	3
4	61	3	3	0	0
5	31	2	2	0	1
6	27	2	2	0	1
7	42	3	3	0	0
8	60	3	3	0	0
9	05	0	0	0	3
10	12	1	1	0	2
11	48	3	3	0	0
12	71	4	3	1	0
13	91	5	3	2	0
14	84	4	3	1	0
15	17	1	1	0	2
16	04	0	0	0	3
17	36	2	2	0	1
18	14	1	1	0	2
19	50	3	3	0	0
20	23	2	2	0	1

From a very short simulation, on only three days are machines not
repaired. On eight of the days the maintenance crews are fully
utilised. Other calculations can be obtained from the simulation.

3. Allocating random numbers in proportion to the frequencies of occurrence:

Customer arrivals:

Time between arrivals (mins)	Frequency	Cumulative Frequency	R.N.
0.5	2	2	0 - 1
1.0	6	8	2 - 7
1.5	10	18	8 - 17
2.0	25	43	18 - 42
2.5	20	63	43 - 62
3.0	14	77	63 - 76
3.5	10	87	77 - 86
4.0	7	94	87 - 93
4.5	4	98	94 - 97
5.0	2	100	98 - 99
	Total 100		

Service times:

Service time (mins)	Frequency	Cumulative Frequency	R.N.
0.5	15	15	0 - 14
1.0	18	33	15 - 32
1.5	38	71	33 - 70
2.0	16	87	71 - 86
2.5	7	94	87 - 93
3.0	6	100	94 - 99
	Total 100		

Typical simulation

Random number	Time between arrivals (mins)	Cumulative time	Random number	Service - time	Time Serviced	Service time completed	Customer waiting time	Cashier idle time
Commence at zero	0	0	9	0.5		0.5	0	0
09	1.5	1.5	76	2.0	1.5	3.5	0	1.0
76	3.0	4.5	58	1.5	4.5	6.0	0	1.0
65	3.0	7.5	73	2.0	7.5	9.5	0	1.5
68	3.0	10.5	26	1.0	10.5	11.5	0	1.0
32	2.0	12.5	62	1.5	12.5	14.0	0	1.0
05	1.0	13.5	27	1.0	14.0	15.0	0.5	
20	2.0	15.5	69	1.5	15.0	16.5	0.5	
23	2.0	17.5	02	0.5	17.5	18.0	0	2.0
43	2.5	20.0	92	2.5	20.0	22.5	0	2.0
50	2.5	22.5	68	1.5	22.5	24.0	0	
25	2.0	24.5	09	0.5	24.5	25.0	0	0.5
34	2.0	26.5	76	2.0	26.5	28.5	0	1.5
71	3.0	29.5	65	1.5	30.0	31.5	0	1.0
30	2.0	31.5	68	1.5	31.5	33.0	0	
97	4.5	36.0	32	1.0	36.0	37.0	0	3.0
						Total	1.0	14.5

Conclusion: Customer waiting time is such that it can be ignored and the cashiers' idle time is approximately 1 minute per customer.

NB. PLEASE NOTE ERROR IN LINE 8!

113

Applications

1. INTERNATIONAL RELIEF ORGANISATION

Relief work was being undertaken in a South American country and, although the immediate emergency was over, it was anticipated that the distribution of food would continue for a considerable time.

Food was being pilfered at an alarming rate due to major problems in organising adequate security at the storage depots and an increasing black market. The situation was becoming serious because of this.

It was decided that the procedure of distribution in the future would be that the foodstuffs would be landed at one prt and stored in a special warehouse that had been recently completed. From here, on the receipt of an official request order, the food would then be transported to five strategically placed depots. Security could be improved by using this method and there would be a better control on food distribution.

Special lorries would be required for distribution, these were to have freezing facilities and specially designed cabs for drivers, to cater for the long distances travelled. The trucks are very expensive and are produced in two sizes, the 'JUNIOR' capable of transporting 500 units or standard containers, and the 'SENIOR' which can accommodate 1,000 containers.

The International Relief Organisation wished to undertake an assignment to find out how many of each type of lorry would be required for the distribution of the standard food containers (often called UNITS) to the five depots.

The distances of the depots from the port were:

Depots	Distances (miles)
Sao Paul	300
Belohor	250
Portoale	600
Salavado	900
Curita	500

A similar situation regarding the distribution of food had arisen several years before and, by careful adjustment to the present population figures, a reasonable estimate could be made of the number of orders which would be received each day at the central port depot.

114

Number of orders per day	Probability of receiving an order
0	2
1	4
2	10
3	15
4	18
5	18
6	16
7	11
8	3
9	1
10	1
11	1

Twelve different sizes of order were possible and the probability of these orders being received from the five depots were estimated to be as shown in the following table:

Depot	Probability or percentage
Sao Paul	40
Belohor	25
Portoale	20
Salavado	10
Curita	5

The probability of the size of order from any of the five depots was found to be:

Size of order	Percentage probability				
	Sao Paul	Belohor	Portoale	Salavado	Curita
20	-	1	1	4	-
50	-	5	9	8	-
100	1	7	10	28	1
200	3	11	10	5	3
300	5	10	5	5	5
400	10	10	5	5	10
500	30	26	20	5	30
600	10	10	4	4	4
700	10	3	6	6	5
800	10	4	7	10	12
900	10	3	7	10	10
1 000	11	10	16	10	20

Although the orders request delivery on a particular date, it was agreed that delivery could be made on either the day before or the day after the actual requested date to give a certain flexibility. Deliveries to Sao Paul and Belohor can be undertaken in one day, which enables the lorries to be considered for deliveries the following day. For Portoale and Curita the delivery and return journey takes two days, and for Salavado three days.

Because of the system of roads deliveries can be made to one depot only, then the lorry has to return to base for further loading and subsequent delivery to any depot allocated.

The lorries are utilised seven days a week, although drivers are allowed one free day off work each week.

The two types of vehicles mentioned are the only ones suitable for this type of work, because of the difficult terrain and their capabilities regarding special food storage. The difference in cost between the models is considerable and they are in short supply.

It is necessary to find the required number of lorries of each model to satisfy demand, within the constraints given.

State your recommendations using Monte Carlo simulation.

Discussion

From a simulation covering thirty days, would it be possible to make the statement that four large and three small lorries only would be sufficient?

Because of road conditions, from experience gained over several years, a minor service to the lorries was necessary at approximately every 2,500 miles, which takes one full day. A major service was necessary every 5,000 miles, which takes two days. Even with this regular servicing breakdowns occur and these were found to be at an average of one lorry per week, resulting in the lorry being out of service for three days.

Consider the effect of these problems on the simulation and how these could be incorporated.

The International Relief Organisation requires figures regarding the running costs of the lorries. It was agreed that for the Senior it cost 12 cruzeiro (local currency) per mile, and for the Junior model, 8 cruzeiro per mile. Excluding servicing and breakdown, what estimated cost could be put forward as an approximate yearly figure? What other factors could be incorporated in the simulation?

2. THE STANDARDISED BOX GROUP

Although the Group produced standard cardboard containers or boxes, an important part of the Group's work was also in printing.

Two particular machines were used for packing and binding standard containers, that had been produced by the Group with their own printing information sheets, which were used for export. Each of the machines had been purchased several years ago and would be extremely expensive to replace. Both machines did the same operation, but machine A took six minutes and machine B took fourteen minutes to pack and bind.

Over time it had been possible to ignore the difference in the speed of completing the work by the machine, due to a steady flow with little delay. Without purchasing new equipment it was not possible to improve on the existing method and, with an estimated increase in the flow of work, more information on machine utilisation and arrival rates of boxes would be required together with any size of queue.

Knowing that the rates of arrival of the boxes were random, it was suggested that a simulation over a period of one hour would be sufficient at the present time to obtain the figures required.

A procedure on the method of obtaining the necessary information was requested, together with the one hour simulation.

Data required for the simulation is listed as follows:

Machine processing time:

Machine	Minutes to complete packing of one standard box
A	6
B	14

The intervals between the arrival of the boxes forms the following frequency distribution:

Interval (mins)	Frequency (%)
4	40
5	30
6	15
7	5
8	5
9	3
10	2

The percentage utilisation of machines A and B are required, together with the maximum size of the queue.

Discussion

Before undertaking the simulation, a plan to increase the production
had been put forward and it was now necessary for the packaging
and binding section to have a total output of 13 boxes. The reaction
to the plan was that the production control section stated that this
figure could not be achieved, even though it would be possible to
increase the speed of production on each machine by the following
amounts:

     Machine A - 30 seconds.
     Machine B - 1 minute.

Would it be possible to achieve the new target with the improved
machine times? Other conditions remain the same.

   Future company plans included modificaitons that would affect the
arrival times of the boxes to the packing and binding section. The
modifications would result in the following times:

Interval (mins)	Frequency (%)
4	50
5	36
6	5
7	4
8	2
9	2
10	1

With the new machine times of five-and-a-half minutes and thirteen
minutes, together with the modified box arrival times, it was
estimated that a new target of fifteen completed boxes could be
achieved per hour. A zero queue was also expected.

Discuss both these assumptions made by the management.

3. IDEAL HOMES (CONSTRUCTION) CORPORATION

The Corporation was developing many sites in areas close to a major city for houses that were selling for between £15,000 and £35,000, depending on design and locality.

The most modern techniques and materials were used in developing the sites and close control was kept on completion dates. However, with the increase in the number of sites to be serviced with equipment, problems had arisen with certain types of machinery not being available when required, causing delays in completion dates.

Modern diggers used for foundation work were shared between several sites. These were sent out from a central depot to the particular site that required them, for varying periods of time. The time taken to complete any one job is measured in multiples of one day.

Although the diggers were mainly used for foundation work, the Corporation found them invaluable for other types of activity. The activities which require this type of equipment arise in a random fashion on the various sites involved. The demand for the digging machinery arising in any one day can be based on the following data, which has been obtained from records over a period of 400 working days.

Table 1

Number of new jobs arising in any one day (x)	Frequency of occurrence (f)
0	130
1	110
2	80
3	50
4	20
5	10
	400

The activities involving the use of the diggers vary in the time taken to complete. The completion time actually approximates that of a negative exponential distribution, but the important figure is that of the mean, which is five days. The distribution of completion times is described by the following:

Table 2

Time to complete job (days)	Probability of time occuring
1	.190
2	.160
3	.120
4	.100
5	.085
6	.065
7	.055
8	.045
9	.034
10	.030
11	.024
12	.019
13	.016
14	.012
15	.010
16	.008
17	.007
18	.006
19	.005
20	.004
21	.005

From time to time there is a heavy demand for the diggers and
therefore the Corporation wishes to keep a number of these available
which could then be shared between the various sites. The equipment
is very expensive to purchase and therefore a correct holding number
of diggers is required.

The Corporation based the number of diggers that would be required
on the following calculations:

From Table 1 the average number of new jobs that arise per day
is calculated:

$$(0 \times 130) + (1 \times 110) + (2 \times 80) + (3 \times 50) + (4 \times 20) + (5 \times 10)$$
$$= \frac{550}{400} \qquad \text{average new job each day} = 1.37.$$

With the average duration time of a job being five days, the
Corporation calculated that the number of diggers required on
average to be shared between the sites would be:

5 x 1.37 = 6.85 items of equipment.

A decision to hold seven diggers was considered satisfactory.

The manager responsible for this work was not entirely convinced that by holding seven diggers at the central depot the work could be completed on time, and that they would be available when required by the various sites. An investigation was requested by him to test the likely consequences of the decision to hold seven diggers.

Assuming that the length of time to complete a job includes the time to deliver the equipment from the depot to the site, plus the time to return the equipment to the depot so that it is available for the next job, carry out the investigation using simulation. Comment on the decision to hold seven units and make your own recommendations.

Discussion

At the Head Office of the Corporation where the final report on the seven diggers was to be forwarded, a request was sent to the local branch for a full report on the consequences of holding six diggers. The percentage of under and/or over utilisation possibilities was to be clearly shown. Study the effects of this new holding figure.

Solutions to applications

1. INTERNATIONAL RELIEF ORGANISATION

Random numbers would be allocated to the distribution, giving the probability of receiving a certain number of orders each day. The same procedure of allocating random numbers would be applied to the distribution of depots from where the order was sent and to each depot, to enable to size of order to be determined.

Table 1
Number of Orders

Number of orders each day	Probability of receiving an order (%)	R.N.
0	2	0 - 1
1	4	2 - 5
2	10	6 - 15
3	15	16 - 30
4	18	31 - 48
5	18	49 - 66
6	16	67 - 82
7	11	83 - 93
8	3	94 - 96
9	1	97
10	1	98
11	1	99

Table 2
Depots

Depot	Probability or percentage	R.N.
Sao Paul	40	0 - 39
Belohor	25	40 - 64
Portoale	20	65 - 84
Salavado	10	85 - 94
Curita	5	95 - 99

Table 3
Order Size

Size of order	Sao Paul	R.N.	Belohor	R.N.	Portoale	R.N.	Salavado	R.N.	Curita	R.N.
20	-	-	1	0	1	0	4	0 - 3	-	-
50	-	-	5	1 - 4	9	1 - 8	8	4 - 11	-	-
100	1	0	2	5 - 12	10	9 - 19	28	12 - 39	1	0
200	3	1 - 3	11	13 - 23	10	20 - 29	5	40 - 44	3	1 - 3
300	5	4 - 8	10	24 - 33	5	30 - 34	5	45 - 49	5	4 - 8
400	10	9 - 18	10	34 - 43	5	35 - 39	5	50 - 54	10	9 - 18
500	30	19 - 48	26	44 - 69	20	40 - 59	5	55 - 59	30	19 - 48
600	10	49 - 58	10	70 - 79	4	60 - 63	4	60 - 63	4	49 - 52
700	10	59 - 68	3	80 - 82	6	64 - 69	6	64 - 69	5	53 - 57
800	10	69 - 78	4	83 - 86	7	70 - 76	10	70 - 79	12	58 - 69
900	10	79 - 88	3	87 - 89	7	77 - 83	10	80 - 89	10	70 - 79
1000	11	89 - 99	10	90 - 99	16	84 - 99	10	90 - 99	20	80 - 99

A typical simulation covering a nine day period is shown in Table 4.

Commencing at day 1, the number of orders received is obtained by sampling from the distribution Table 1. Random number 7 signifies that two orders were received. Sampling from Table 2 will enable the destination to be obtained and random numbers 42 and 31 signify that the orders were from Belohor and Sao Paul respectively. To obtain the size of these orders we sample from Table 3. With random numbers 17 and 60 the size of orders for Belohor and Sao Paul will be 200 and 700 respectively.

We now consider what size of lorry would be suitable for delivery. Designate S_1, S_2, S_3 to represent small lorries 1, 2 and 3, and L_1, L_2, L_3, etc. to represent large lorries 1, 2 and 3 etc.

The delivery of 200 units to Belohor could be undertaken by a 500 unit (small) lorry shown as S_1. The mileage will be 250 miles to Belohor and 250 miles return journey, giving 500 miles total, entered under column S_1.

Brackets indicate where it has been possible to combine loads to give a reasonable untilisation of the lorry loads.

By designating the lorries with S_x and L_x it is possible to schedule when the lorries return from their assignments and are available for further deliveries.

By counting the numbers of S_x and L_x at the end of the simulation the total number of small and large lorries required can be obtained. In this small simulation, four small lorries are indicated S_1, S_2, S_3, and S_4, and four large lorries L_1, L_2, L_3 and L_4.

124

Table 4

International Relief Organisation: Typical Simulation

Day	R.N.	Number of Orders	R.N.	Destination	R.N.	Size of Order	Type of lorry (S = Small, L = Large)	S_1	S_2	S_3	S_4	S_5	L_1	L_2	L_3	L_4	L_5
								Cumulative lorry mileage									
1	7	2	42	Belohor	17	200	S_1	500									
			31	Sao Paul	60	700)	L_1						600				
2	22	3	3	Sao Paul	4	300)	S_1	1,000									
			51	Belohor	52	500	S_2		1,800								
			90	Salavado	21	100											
3	80	6	16	Sao Paul	97	1,000	L_1						1,200				
			3	Sao Paul	2	200)											
			19	Sao Paul	72	800)	L_2							600			
			36	Sao Paul	4	300	S_1	1,600									
			69	Portoale	78	900	L_3								1,200		
			15	Sao Paul	77	800	L_4									600	
4	91	7	17	Sao Paul	22	500	S_1	2,200									
			49	Belohor	45	500)	L_1						1,700				
			15	Sao Paul	16	400)											
			4	Sao Paul	32	500)	L_2							1,200			
			23	Sao Paul	23	500	S_3			600							
			70	Portoale	38	400)	L_4									1,800	
			74	Portoale	27	200)											
5	89	7	65	Portoale	49	500	S_1	3,400									
			28	Sao Paul	12	400	S_2		2,400								
			31	Sao Paul	99	1,000	L_2							1,800			

Table 4 (cont)

Day	R.N.	Number of Orders	R.N.	Destination	R.N.	Size of Order	Type of lorry S = Small L = Large	S_1	S_2	S_3	S_4	S_5	L_1	L_2	L_3	L_4	L_5
												Cumulative lorry mileage					
5 (cont)			18	Sao Paul	65	700	L_3 split								1,800		
			49	Belohor	17	200	L_1 combine										
			04	Sao Paul	70	800	S_3 split			1,200							
			42	Belohor	29	300	S_4				500						
6	51	5	50	Belohor	18	200	L_1 combine										
			20	Sao Paul	27	500	L_2							2,400			
			94	Salavado	45	300	S_2 combine		4,300								
			93	Salavado	04	50											
			44	Belohor	77	600	L_1 combine						2,200				
7	7	2	9	Sao Paul	16	400	L_2							3,000			
			51	Belohor	32	300	S_3 combine			1,700							
8	15	2	23	Sao Paul	70	800	L_2 combine							3,600			
			38	Sao Paul	17	400	L_1										
9	49	5	16	Sao Paul	50	600	L_1 combine						2,800				
			3	Sao Paul	20	500	S_3			2,300							
			19	Sao Paul	65	700	L_3								2,400		
			36	Sao Paul	17	400	S_2		4,800								
			97	Curita	45	500	S_1	4,400									

2. THE STANDARDISED BOX GROUP

Procedure

(a) Make an allocation of numbers between 0 and 99 to each interval of arrivals in proportion to the frequency of that particular interval.

(b) From a random number table extract a list of numbers.

(c) Use this list to simulate the arrival of boxes into the section.

(d) Place each box in sequence on:

    (i) machine A if not utilised;

    (ii) machine B if machine A is utilised;

    (iii) place in queue if both A and B are engaged.

(e) Continue the simulation for sixty minutes and calculate the percentage utilisation of each machine and the maximum size of the queue.

Allocating random numbers 0 - 99 to the intervals between arrivals:

Interval (mins)	Frequency (%)	Random numbers
4	40	0 - 39
5	30	40 - 69
6	15	70 - 84
7	5	85 - 89
8	5	90 - 94
9	3	95 - 97
10	2	98 - 99

Extracting a list of random numbers:

41, 17, 31, 30, 14, 76, 93, 88, 89, 28, 71.

This gives the intervals in minutes as:

5, 4, 4, 4, 4, 6, 8, 7, 7, 4, 6,

with the arrival times of:

0, 5, 9, 13, 17, 21, 27, 35, 42, 49, 53, 59.

The simulation for the sixty minutes is shown in Table 1. We assume the simulation will commence on the arrival of the first box.

Table 1
Simulation of Packaging and Binding

Conditions of Machines

Time (mins)	Arrival of box	A U = utilised	B UN = unutilised	Length of the queue
1	1	U 1 - 6	UN 1 - 4	0
5	2		U 5 - 18	0
7		UN 7 - 8		0
9	3	U 9 - 14		0
13	4			1
		U 15 - 20		0
17	5			1
19			U 19 - 32	0
21	6	U 21 - 26		0
27	7	U 27 - 32		0
33		UN 33 - 34	UN 33 - 41	0
35	8	U 35 - 40		0
41		UN 41		0
42	9	U 42 - 47	UN 42 - 52	0
48		UN 48		0
49	10	U 49 - 54		0
53	11		U 53 - 66	0
55		UN 55 - 58		0
59	12	U 59 - 64		0

The percentage utilisation of Machine A is $\dfrac{50}{60}$ or 83%

The percentage utilisation of Machine B is $\dfrac{36}{60}$ or 60%

The maximum size of the queue is 1.

3. IDEAL HOMES (CONSTRUCTION) CORPORATION

Allocate random numbers to frequency of occurrency in Table 1.

Table 1

Number of new jobs arising in any one day	Frequency of occurrence	Cumulative %	R.N.
0	130	32.5	000 - 324
1	110	60.0	325 - 599
2	80	80.0	600 - 799
3	50	92.5	800 - 924
4	20	97.5	925 - 974
5	10	100.0	975 - 999

Allocate random numbers to probabilities in Table 2.

Table 2

Time to complete job (days)	Probability of time occuring	Cumulative %	R.N.
1	.190	19.0	000 - 189
2	.160	35.0	190 - 349
3	.120	47.0	350 - 469
4	.100	57.0	470 - 569
5	.085	65.5	570 - 654
6	.065	72.0	650 - 719
7	.055	77.5	720 - 774
8	.045	82.0	775 - 819
9	.034	85.4	820 - 883
10	.030	88.4	854 - 883
11	.024	90.8	884 - 907
12	.019	92.7	908 - 926
13	.016	94.3	927 - 942
14	.012	95.5	943 - 954
15	.010	96.5	955 - 964
16	.008	97.3	965 - 972
17	.007	98.0	973 - 979
18	.006	98.6	980 - 985
19	.005	99.1	986 - 990
20	.004	99.5	991 - 994
21	.005	100.0	995 - 999

Procedure

We will assume that no jobs are outstanding to commence the simulation, entered in column 2 for day 1. To obtain the number of new jobs received, we sample from Table 1. Obtain random number and enter in column 3, (201). This represents zero jobs received and this is

129

entered in column 4. Thus all diggers are available but not utilised, the spaces are therefore left blank in column 7.

For day 2 there are zero jobs outstanding and this is entered under column 2. Random number (744) represents two new jobs, we sample from Table 2 and obtain random numbers (558) and (672), representing the duration times of four and six days respectively. These are entered in column 6.

Two diggers will be required for the times stated and these periods are designated under column 7. The remaining spaces are left blank, as the remaining five diggers are not utilised. The procedure is repeated for day 3 and so on.

Note that at day 5 two of the jobs requiring six days duration cannot be carried out because no diggers are available. Day 6 therefore shows that there are two jobs outstanding. Two diggers are available on day 6, therefore these outstanding jobs can be carried out, however, it is not possible to cater for the new job and this is marked with an asterisk.

The number of outstanding jobs can be obtained from column 2 and the blank spaces under column 7 will show where the diggers are not being utilised. There are other variations which could be included in the simulation.

For the simulation carried out for a period of 24 days, there are 7 x 24 = 168 machine-days available and the number of blank spaces showing non-utilisation = 42.

Non-utilisation of plant = $\dfrac{42}{168}$ x 100 = 25%

Jobs outstanding over 24 days = 8 out of 28, but they rarely have to wait longer than one day.

A much longer simulation would be required to form any definite conclusions. Indications are that there are sufficient diggers available to meet present demand if a delay to commence outstanding jobs of one day is satisfactory.

Ideal Homes (Construction) Corporation: Typical Simulation

Day No. (1)	Jobs Outstanding (2)	R.N. (3)	New Jobs (4)	Random Numbers (5)					Job Duration (days) (6)					Digger Numbers (7)						
				1	2	3	4	5	1	2	3	4	5	1	2	3	4	5	6	7
1	0	201	0																	
2	0	744	2	558	672				4	6										
3	0	947	4	858	401	945	116		10	3	14	1								
4	0	221	0																	
5	0	932	4	640	509	669	669		5	4	6*	6*								
6	2	450	1	335					2*											
7	1	449	1	524					4*											
8	2	162	0																	
9	1	045	0																	
10	0	327	1	749					7											
11	0	036	0																	
12	0	624	2	502	494				4	4										
13	0	610	2	196	641				2	5										
14	0	890	3	184	655	799			1	6*	8*									
15	2	017	0																	
16	0	275	0																	
17	0	490	1	072					1											
18	0	497	1	900					11											
19	0	202	0																	
20	0	488	1	538					4											
21	0	087	0																	
22	0	959	4	981	089	372	422		18	1	3	3								
23	0	379	1	044					1											
24	0	057	0																	

6 Linear programming

Management is usually faced with restrictions on the amount of money available for expansion and the purchase of new equipment. Restrictions on the number of hours available on a particular machine and whether the required number of labour hours can be obtained also cause many problems.

With an objective of obtaining maximum profit or minimum costs within the restrictions mentioned, linear programming models can be formulated. However, the term 'linear' implies proportionality such as, if one machine takes one hour to produce one article it takes two hours for the completion of two articles and the cost of material for one component is 50p then two will cost £1. In some problems this linearity does not exist and yet it can often be possible to break down the particular problem into parts and use linear programming. An example of this is, a skilled worker earned £22 per day, this was for a total of ten hours' work, which for our linear purposes is £2.20 per hour, giving £22 total. However, the total amount is made up of eight normal hours at £2 per hour, and two hours overtime at £3 per hour. By breaking up the hours into two parts we get the 'true' situation and proportionality.

A linear programming type of problem which can be solved graphically enables many basic principles to be studied.

EXAMPLE 1

A company manufactures two machines called 'Standard' and 'Deluxe'. Each of the machines has to be processed through three stages, which we could call A, B and C. One Standard machine requires four hours through A, ten hours through B, and 12 hours through C. The Deluxe machine requires four hours through A, ten hours through B, and four hours through C. The number of hours that are available on the machines for this work is 48 hours on A, 88 hours on B and 120 hours on C. The profit per machine is £120 for the Standard and £180 for the Deluxe model. The machines can be made available when required and we wish to know how many of each model should be produced to give maximum profit.

Even with a simple problem such as the one presented, it is often very helpful to draw the problem using a 'systems' approach.

PROCESSES

Product	A	B	C	Profit
Standard	4	2	12	£120
Deluxe	4	10	4	£180
Hours available	48	88	120	

We need to formulate the problem into a linear model:

Let X be the number of Standard units produced;
Let Y be the number of Deluxe units produced.

To produce 1 unit of X requires 4 hours of A;
To produce 1 unit of Y requires 4 hours of A;
Total hours available on A is 48.

Although we cannot have more than 48 hours, we do not wish to restrict the problem any more than necessary and therefore algebraically we use an inequality sign less than or equal to $\leq$.

$4X + 4Y \leq 48.$

Process B is restricted to 88 hours with X requiring 2 hours and Y requiring 10 hours:

$2X + 10Y \leq 88.$

Process C is restricted to 120 hours with X requiring 12 hours and Y requiring 4 hours:

$12X + 4Y \leq 120.$

It is not possible to produce negative quantities of X and Y, therefore,

$X \geq 0$

$X \geq 0.$

In this instance our objective is to maximise profit and we can obtain £120 each for X and £180 for Y, therefore $120X + 180Y$ is to be a maximum and is the 'objective function'. Gathering all the terms together we have:

Maximise		120X	+	180Y			_____ (1)
Subject to		4X	+	4Y	$\leq$	48	
		2X	+	10Y	$\leq$	88	_____ (2)
		12X	+	4Y	$\leq$	120	
and		X	$\geq$	0			_____ (3)
		Y	$\geq$	0			

Thus any pair of values of X and Y which will satisfy the inequalities of (2) and (3) is called a 'feasible' solution but an 'optimal' solution is a feasible solution which will also satisfy (1)

As we are only considering two variables X and Y the problem can be shown graphically, problems containing more than two variables will be discussed later in the chapter.

The equation 4X + 4Y = 48 defines a straight line and we can obtain the points where this line cuts the X and Y axis by letting X = 0 and finding the value of Y and repeating for Y = 0 and finding the value of X. We are interested in the equation 4X + 4Y ≤ 48 and values of X and Y which will give a feasible solution will be found on the boundaries of the area A, B, C or to the left of AB.

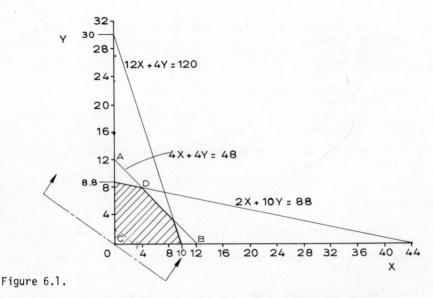

Figure 6.1.

Similar lines are drawn for 2X + 10Y = 88 and 12X + 4Y = 120, which are shown plotted on Figure 6.1. Values that will give a feasible solution will be either on or to the left of the plotted lines, therefore the feasible area is that shaded.

Our objective is to maximise 120X + 180Y, therefore let 120X + 180Y equal any amount to obtain a line to fit the equation. The coefficients denote the angle of slope therefore for convenience of arithmetic let 120X + 180Y = 360. Therefore, when X = 0, Y = 2 and when Y = 0, X = 3.

The profit slope is drawn as shown in Figure 6.1, giving zero profit and cutting the origin. We require a parallel line to this to be as far away as possible from zero without violating the restrictions and moving into a 'non feasible' area. The point farthest from zero that the line will cut without any violation of restrictions is at D.

134

Reading off the drawing we find that at this point Y = 8 and X = 4 and by substituting in the objective function 120X + 180Y we obtain (120 x 4) + (180 x 8) = 480 + 1,440 = £1,920 by producing 8 Deluxe and 4 Standard units.

This is a unique solution in that only at point D will all the restrictions be satisfied

In this example the slope of the objective function did not correspond to any slope of the restrictions and therefore only one answer became possible. If an objective function slope corresponds to that of a restriction, it means that any point along that slope and extreme ends would satisfy the objective functions, thus alternative solutions exist.

If we substitute for X and Y in the various equations other information can be obtained. Restriction on process A was 4X + 4Y ≤ 48 thus the number of hours required was (4 x 4) + (4 x 8) = 48 hours and therefore this process would be fully utilised. Restriction on process B was 2X + 10Y ≤ 88, thus the number of hours required was (2 x 4) + (10 x 8) = 88, again fully utilised. The final restriction was on process C, 12X + 4Y ≤ 120 and the requirements (12 x 4) + (4 x 8) = 80 hours. Thus for process C, 40 hours of the 120 available are not required and could be used for other work if necessary.

If our objective function concerned minimising costs, which by taking the previous example will now read that costs to produce a Standard unit is £120 and a Deluxe unit £180 and all other factors remain the same, the problem differs slightly. We now wish to know how many to produce of X and Y to give minimum cost.

The formulation of the model gives:

120		120X	+	180Y	=	minimum
subject to		4X	+	4Y	≤	48
		2X	+	10Y	≤	88
		12X	+	4Y	≤	120
and		X			≥	0
		Y			≥	0

The slope of the objective function remains the same but in this problem we need to be as near to zero as possible without violating the restriction, Figure 6.2. The nearest point the line touches without entering the non-feasible area is at B where Y = 0 and X = 10, and the total cost would be (120 x 10) + (180 x 0) = £1,200.

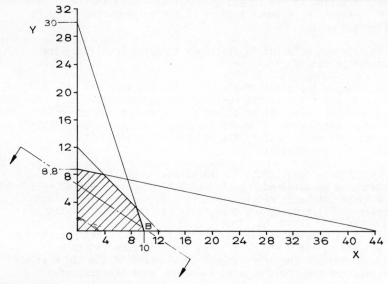

Figure 6.2.

The number of hours required:

Process A	(4 x 10)	+	(4 x 0)	=	40 hours
Process B	(2 x 10)	+	(10 x 0)	=	20 hours
Process C	(12 x 10)	+	(4 x 0)	=	120 hours

only Process C would be fully utilised.

If we take an even simpler problem which can be solved graphically, the figures can be used for an algebraic interpretation and the methods adopted for Simplex.

EXAMPLE 2.

A company manufactures two articles which we will designate X and Y. Each article is processed through two stages, A and B, and the processing time with hours available is as follows:

Process

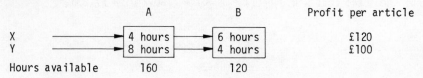

	A	B	Profit per article
X	4 hours	6 hours	£120
Y	8 hours	4 hours	£100
Hours available	160	120	

How many of each article should be produced to give maximum profit?

136

Problem formulation

Maximum (objective function)   120X + 100Y   _____(1)

subject to $4X + 8Y \leq 160$ _____(2)
                                 $6X + 4Y \leq 120$ _____(3)

and $X \geq 0$ _____(4)
                                 $Y \geq 0$ _____(5)

The problem presented graphically is shown in Figure 6.3.

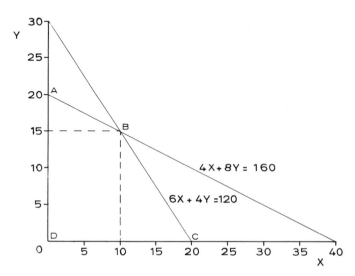

Figure 6.3.

From the figure it can be seen that at point B the combination of
X and Y gives the greatest profit. By producing 10 of X and 15 of Y
the profit is (10 x 120) + (15 x 100) = £2,700.

DEVELOPMENT OF AN ALGEBRAIC SOLUTION

Reviewing equations (2) and (3) in Example 2, these are inequalities
and state that a combination of X and Y hours must not exceed 160 hours
on A and 120 hours on process B. It is possible that there could be
idle time and if we let S_A represent this in equation (2) we obtain:

$4X + 8Y + S_A = 160$ _____(6)

For process B:

$6X + 4Y + S_B = 120$ _____(7)

137

We can ignore negative values for S_A and S_B as negative production and idle time is not possible.

We now have two equations with four unknowns and we wish to obtain values for X, Y, S_A and S_B. It can be shown that there is a solution to the problem, such that at least two of the unknowns are zero. The problem becomes one of determining which of the two variables should be zero to give the maximum profit.

A first solution:

A feasible solution could be to produce zero, which is the worst, as there would be zero profit. But it enables us to commence and we then require a step by step method that enables us to find the optimum solution.

$$S_A = 160 - 4(X) - 8(Y) \hspace{3cm} (8)$$
$$S_B = 120 - 6(X) - 4(Y) \hspace{3cm} (9)$$

If X and Y are zero then idle time is at a maximum:

$$S_A = 160 - 4(0) - 8(0) = 160 \text{ hours}$$
$$S_B = 120 - 6(0) - 4(0) = 120 \text{ hours}$$

For the objective function

$$\text{Maximum profit} = 120X + 100Y = 120(0) + 100(0) = 0 \underline{\hspace{1cm}} (10)$$

which is as expected, no production and zero profit. This would be represented on Figure 6.3. by point D.

Improving the first solution:

It would be to our advantage to reduce S_A and S_B towards zero and select X or Y with a positive value. The problem is which variable X or Y should be chosen to give up the largest figure.

By looking at the objective function, each unit of X earns £120 and each unit of Y earns £100. Therefore we need to increase X from 0 to some positive value.

Knowing the maximum number of hours available on each process we need to make X as large as possible without violating the restrictions. Taking equation (6) the maximum possible for X is when S_A and Y is zero.

$$X = \frac{160 - (8 \times 0) - 0}{4} = 40 \hspace{3cm} (11)$$

Taking equation (7) we obtain:

$$X = \frac{120 - (4 \times 0) - 0}{6} = 20 \hspace{3cm} (12)$$

Equation (7) is called the controlling equation because the value of X greater than 20 is not permitted. We will increase X to the maximum and also reduce S_B to zero. The two variables having positive values will now be X and S_A, Y and S_B will be zero. The controlling equation (7) is used for solving for X.

$$X = \frac{120 - 4Y - S_B}{6}$$

$$X = 20 - \frac{2Y}{3} - \frac{S_B}{6} \qquad \qquad \underline{\hspace{2cm}}(13)$$

This expression of X limits it to the maximum possible value, therefore we will substitute this expression in (6) and in the objective function (10):

$$S_A = 160 - 4(20 - \frac{2Y}{3} - \frac{S_B}{6}) - 8Y$$

simplifying becomes:

$$S_A = 80 - \frac{16Y}{3} + \frac{2S_B}{3} \qquad \qquad \underline{\hspace{2cm}}(14)$$

substituting (13) in the objective function

$$\text{Maximum profit} = 120(20 - \frac{2Y}{3} - \frac{S_B}{6}) + 100Y$$

$$= 2,400 + 20Y - 20S_B \qquad \qquad \underline{\hspace{2cm}}(15)$$

If we let Y and S_B become zero and substitute these in (13) we can obtain X, with S_A obtained from equation (14):

$$X = 20 \qquad \text{from (13)}$$
$$S_A = 80 \qquad \text{from (14)}$$
$$Y = 0$$
$$S_B = 0$$

Maximum profit = £2,400   from (10).

If we observe Figure 6.3. it is point C that has been reached, which gives the profit of £2,400, and its a much superior solution than at point D, which was our first solution.

To investigate any possible improvement on this figure, observe equation (15). For every additional unit of Y, profit could be increased by £20 plus any decrease in S_B. With S_B already zero, only increasing Y can be considered.

Repeating our previous procedure, how much is it possible to increase Y? Inspecting the equations obtained (13) and (14), from (14) the maximum value of Y occurs when S_A and S_B are zero and Y = 15. From (13) the maximum value of Y is when S_B and X are zero, or Y = 30.

The restricting equation is (14) and therefore becomes the 'controlling equation'. Solve (14) for Y.

$$Y = 15 + \frac{1S_B}{8} - \frac{3S_A}{16} \qquad \underline{\qquad}(16)$$

If we substitute the value of Y in equation (13) and in the latest equation for the objective function (15), we obtain:

$$X = 10 + \frac{1S_A}{8} - \frac{1S_B}{4} \qquad \underline{\qquad}(17)$$

$$\text{Maximum profit} = 2,700 - \frac{15S_A}{4} - \frac{35S_B}{2} \qquad \underline{\qquad}(18)$$

With the values of S_A and S_B being zero the variable values and the objective function become:

$$X = 10$$
$$Y = 15$$
$$S_A = 0$$
$$S_B = 0$$

Maximum profit = £2,700.

If we now look at Figure 6.3. we are at point B which is the point where the pair of values for X and Y gives us the optimum solution. However, from the equation (18) can we tell that the optimum has been reached? Only by decreasing either S_A and S_B or both, can we improve on £2,700. Since both are zero and negative values are not feasible, there is no way in which an improvement can be made. The optimal solution has been achieved.

SIMPLEX METHOD

The graphical method was suitable for a two dimensional model, but becomes somewhat complex for three and the algebraic approach is tedious even for the simple example presented. For more complex models a procedural approach, keeping computation to a minimum is required. Before presenting a suitable method for solving problems of greater complexity it would be to our advantage to examine further what the previous two methods have shown.

The first solution was at point D, the second at C and finally the optimum solution was at point B on Figure 6.3. There are many other points that could have been considered on the perimeter of, and within, the area A, D, C, B, all feasible. The reader can check that all the possible solutions not checked would involve more than two of the four variables as positive values. Only at the points or corners of our two dimensional problem are only two variables positive, the same applies to three or more dimensional problems. We thus jump from corner to corner, increasing or improving on the previous solution until we reach the optimum.

The Simplex method does exactly the same, moving from one point or corner to another, testing each point to see whether an optimum has been reached before proceeding.

The Simplex procedure

For comparison with the two methods discussed, the previous problem will be used to develop the procedure.

Reviewing our previous equations (6) and (7) which were the restricting equations for process A and process B respectively:

$$4X + 8Y + S_A = 160$$
$$6X + 4Y + S_B = 120$$

and the objective function equation (10):

$$120X + 100Y = \text{Maximum profit.}$$

This equation can be rewritten as follows, because S_A and S_B make no contribution to the profit:

$$120X + 100Y + (0)S_A + (0)S_B = \text{Maximum profit.}$$

A table is formed using our equations, with the variables at the head of the columns, the coefficients under the appropriate columns and the constants on the left hand side of the table, with the equality sign removed. A zero in columns S_A and S_B signifies that this particular idle time is not applicable to the process being considered.

	X	Y	S_A	S_B
160	4	8	1	0
120	6	4	0	1

To complete the first Simplex matrix, Table 6.1., we can refer to the algebraic method where the initial solution was to produce zero, with idle time taking the hours available for processing.

Table 6.1.
First Simplex Matrix

			120 X	100 Y	0 S_A	0 S_B
0	S_A	160	4	8	1	0
0	S_B	120	6	4	0	1

On the top row are the coeffi ients that make a contribution to the profit, £120 per unit of X and £100 per unit of Y. The first column showing zeros indicates at any given point in the solution the contribution rates of the variables in the objective function. The second column shows the variables in the solution and the third giving the amounts of the variables in the solution. The same procedure is adopted for all problems of this nature and only the size of the matrix will alter.

As in the algebraic method we consider the possibility of an improvement to the first solution.

We first calculate what we will call an INDEX ROW which forms the bottom row of the matrix, shown in Table 6.2. Note it is merely the top row number of the matrix, with negative signs and indicates the potential improvement or opportunity lost by not introducing the variable into the solution.

When all numbers in this row become zero or positive the optimum solution has been reached. The zero in the third column and index row indicates that no profit has yet been gained.

Table 6.2.
First Simplex Matrix with Index Row

			120 X	100 Y	0 S_A	0 S_B	
0	S_A	160	4	8	1	0	
0	S_B	120	6	4	0	1	
		O	-120	-100	0	0	INDEX ROW

Selection of the Pivot Column and Pivot Row

From Table 6.2. we can see that by introducing variable X into the solution it would give the greatest improvement. The column containing X is denoted the PIVOT COLUMN. With X being introduced in place of either S_A or S_B we select a PIVOT ROW to determine which it will replace. To calculate the PIVOT ROW divide each number in column three by the corresponding positive non-zero number in the PIVOT COLUMN.

The results are compared and the PIVOT ROW is the one which gives the smallest non-negative value. The calculations for the problem under study are:

First Row, $\dfrac{160}{4} = 40$

Second Row, $\dfrac{120}{6} = 20 = $ PIVOT ROW

We are in fact performing the same calculation as in the algebraic method, which is selecting the equation limiting the value of X. See equations (11) and (12).

Where the PIVOT COLUMN and PIVOT ROW intersect, which is at 6, this figure is called the PIVOT KEY. Table 6.3. shows the first Simplex matrix with index row, pivot row, pivot column and pivot key.

Table 6.3.
First Simplex Matrix with Index Row, Pivot Column,
Pivot Row and Pivot Number

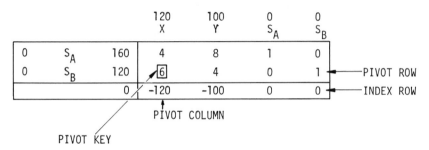

			120 X	100 Y	0 S_A	0 S_B	
0	S_A	160	4	8	1	0	
0	S_B	120	6	4	0	1	──PIVOT ROW
		0	-120	-100	0	0	──INDEX ROW

PIVOT COLUMN

PIVOT KEY

Constructing an improved solution

A new second row is created by dividing through by the PIVOT KEY with the first column figure, showing the contribution rate in the objective function. S_B is replaced by the incoming variable value. Table 6.4. shows the completed calculations.

It should be noted that the values in the new second row, ignoring the sign, are identical with equation (13) which was solving the equation for process B for the variable X.

143

Table 6.4.
First Simplex Matrix with Incoming Variable Value, Contribution Rate and New Row completed

First Matrix			120 X	100 Y	0 S_A	0 S_B
0	S_A	160	4	8	1	0
0	S_B	120	6	4	0	1
		Q	-120	-100	0	0

Second Matrix

0   S_A

| 120 | X | 20 | 1 | $\frac{2}{3}$ | 0 | $\frac{1}{6}$ | new second row |

With the new second row formed the remaining calculations are obtained by using the following formula:

$$\text{NEW NUMBER} = \text{old number} - \frac{(\text{Corresponding no. of Pivot Row}) \times (\text{Corresponding no. of Pivot Column})}{\text{Pivot Key}}$$

1. Third column, first row,

   new number $= 160 - \dfrac{120 \times 4}{6} = 80$

2. Fourth column, first row,

   new number $= 4 - \dfrac{6 \times 4}{6} = 0$

3. Fifth column, first row,

   new number $= 8 - \dfrac{4 \times 4}{6} = 5\frac{1}{3}$

4. Sixth column, first row,

   new number $= 1 - \dfrac{0 \times 4}{6} = 1$

5. Seventh column, first row,

   new number $= 0 - \dfrac{1 \times 4}{6} = -\frac{2}{3}$

These calculations give a new first row in matrix 2 Table 6.5. We will complete the matrix by forming a new index row following the procedure adopted.

1. Third column, third row,

$$\text{new number} = 0 - \frac{120 \times -120}{6} = 2,400$$

2. Fourth column, third row,

$$\text{new number} = -120 - \frac{6 \times -120}{6} = 0$$

3. Fifth column, third row,

$$\text{new number} = -100 - \frac{4 \times -120}{6} = -20$$

4. Sixth column, third row,

$$\text{new number} = 0 - \frac{0 \times +120}{6} = 0$$

5. Seventh column, third row,

$$\text{new number} = 0 - \frac{1 \times -120}{6} = 20$$

Table 6.5.
First and Second Matrix with new rows completed

Matrix 1

			120 X	100 Y	0 S_A	0 S_B
0	S_A	160	4	8	1	0
0	S_B	120	6	4	0	1
		0	-120	-100	0	0

Matrix 2

0	S_A	80	0	$5\frac{1}{3}$	1	$\frac{2}{3}$
120	X	20	1	$\frac{2}{3}$	0	$\frac{1}{6}$
		2,400	0	-20	0	20

In forming a new first and third row we are doing the equivalent of substituting the value of X determined by equation (13) in the equation for process B and in the objective function. Note that the coefficients in the first row, ignoring the sign, are the same as in equation (14) with those in the third row as shown in equation (15).

145

Reviewing Matrix 2, the solution at this stage is:

$$S_A = 80$$
$$X = 20$$
$$Y = 0$$
$$S_B = 0$$

The second column indicates the positive values which are the constants S_A and X and with Y and S_B not entering, these are zero. The maximum profit is indicated as 2,400 in the third row. A -20 in the third row, fifth column, indicates that the solution can be improved by introducing variable Y.

We can now repeat the procedure adopted and with Y being the only negative value, proceed to choose this column as the pivot column. The key row is chosen as before. The two calculations are:

$$\text{First row} = \frac{80}{5\frac{1}{3}} = 15 \quad \text{(Pivot row)}$$

$$\text{Second row} = \frac{20}{\frac{2}{3}} = 30$$

The first row becomes the pivot row and where the pivot column and row intersect is the pivot key. A new first row is developed by dividing through the old first row by the pivot key. Other rows are computed as before and Table 6.6. is formed.

Table 6.6.
First and Second Matrix Completed

Matrix 1

			120 X	100 Y	0 S_A	0 S_B	
0	S_A	160	4	8	1	0	
0	S_B	120	6	4	0	1	◄——Pivot row
		0	-120	-100	0	0	◄——Index row

Pivot key   Pivot column

Matrix 2

			X	Y	S_A	S_B	
0	S_A	80	0	$5\frac{1}{3}$	1	$\frac{2}{3}$	◄——Pivot row
120	X	20	1	$\frac{2}{3}$	0	$\frac{1}{6}$	
		2,400	0	-20	0	20	

Pivot column

146

Table 6.7.
Final Matrix Completed

Matrix 3			120 X	100 Y	0 S_A	0 S_B
100	Y	15	0	1	$\frac{3}{16}$	$-\frac{1}{8}$
120	X	10	1	0	$-\frac{1}{8}$	$\frac{1}{4}$
		2,700	0	0	$3\frac{3}{4}$	$17\frac{1}{2}$

No negative values exist in the third row therefore an optimum value has been reached. The values of the variables for the optimal solution are:

Y = 15

X = 10

S_A = 0

S_B = 0

Maximum profit = £2,700.

The values are the same as found by the graphical and algebraic methods.

Interpretation of the final table

1. The interpretation of the optimum solution is as follows:

   (a) The solution appears in the first three columns. Column one contains the value of the variable introduced into the solution, the second column contains that variable and column three the variable quantity. All variables that do not appear here are equal to zero.

2. The bottom row can be interpreted as follows:

   (a) The number in the third column is the value of the objective function for the solution represented.

   (b) A negative number in this row indicates the algebraic increase in the objective function if one unit of the variable at the head of the column was introduced into the solution.

   (c) A positive number in the index row indicates the algebraic reduction in the objective function if one unit of the variable at the head of that column was introduced into the solution.

   (d) Where the variable at the head of the column is a process, a positive value in the index row has much the same meaning as in (c) above. However, it may also be thought of as representing 'opportunity profit' or the amount of algebraic increase possible in the objective function if one more unit of the variable heading that column were available in the first solution: i.e. if the restraint of the problem were relaxed by one unit.

3. The remaining numbers in the matrix represent the marginal rate of exchange between the variables in the row and column at the particular solution represented.

   (a) A positive rate of exchange indicates the decrease in the variables in that row that results with the addition of one unit of the variable in that column.

   (b) A negative rate of exchange indicates the increase in the variable in that row that results with the addition of one unit of the variable in that column.

It would be appropriate the summarise the procedure adopted for deriving solutions by the Simplex technique.

Summary of procedure

1. Formulate the problem and the objective function.

2. Convert the inequation to equations by adding a different non-negative variable called IDLE time to each.

3. Set up the table of the coefficients of the restrictions.

4. Write the negatives of the profit in the bottom row.

5. Select the PIVOT COLUMN, this has the most negative number in the bottom row.

6. Select the PIVOT ROW, this has the smallest non-negative value, obtianed by dividing the figures in the third column by the equivalent figure in the PIVOT COLUMN.

7. Select the PIVOT KEY, this is the figure at the intersection of the PIVOT COLUMN and the PIVOT ROW.

8. Develop a new row for the old row containing the PIVOT KEY which is formed by

$$\frac{\text{NEW ROW}}{\text{NUMBER}} = \frac{\text{EACH NUMBER IN THE PIVOT ROW OF PRECEDING TABLE}}{\text{PIVOT KEY}}$$

9. Develop the remainder of the table:

   (a) The objective number and variable at the head of the PIVOT COLUMN are entered in the first and second columns respectively of the new row. These replace the variable and objective number from the PIVOT ROW in the preceding table.

148

(b) The remainder of the variable and objective columns are reproduced in the new table exactly as they were in the preceding table.

(c) The remainder of the coeffeicients for the new table are calculated by the formula:

$$\text{New number} = \text{Old number} - \frac{(\text{Corresponding number of Pivot Row}) \times (\text{Corresponding number of Pivot Column})}{\text{Pivot Key}}$$

10. Repeat steps 5 through to 9(c) until all the figures in the bottom row are non-negative. When this point has been reached an optimum solution then results.

Further extensions to the Simplex method exist and references to these are made in the bibliography. See number (44) and number (46).

EXERCISES

1. A sheet metal company are producing two types of steel shelving, I and II. Each type I shelving requires 20 square feet of 22 gauge sheet steel and 30 feet of $\frac{1}{4}$-inch metal rods, together with six man hours of labour. Each type II requires 30 square feet of 22 gauge sheet steel and 30 feet of $\frac{1}{4}$-inch metal rods with labour of four man hours.

The profit of each type of cabinet I is £3.00, and for type II, £3.60. A promise to supply 40 type I shelves in the coming month must be kept. In the coming month 2,400 square feet of 22 gauge sheet metal and 2,700 feet of $\frac{1}{4}$-inch metal rodding, together with 480 man hours will be available.

How many of each type of shelving should be produced to give the maximum profit?

2. A company manufactures two types of chairs, type A and type B. Both types have to pass through three processes and the time for each process per unit is given in the following table:

	Shaping Dept.	Setting Dept.	Finishing Dept.
Type A	3.6 hours	6 hours	3 hours
Type B	4 hours	4 hours	4 hours

The profit made on the sale of type A is £10 per unit and for type B £12.50. The total available monthly capacity for each department is 3,600 hours.

(a) Assuming that the company can sell all that are manufactured, how many of each type should be produced to give maximum profit?

(b) If there were only sufficient materials to produce either 625 units of type A, or 500 units of type B per month, how would this affect your product mix?

(c) If a late sales forecast sets an upper sales limit of 250 of type A and also of type B per month, what would your policy be for manufacturing?

150

3. A manufacturing department produces two styles of product, A and B. Both styles pass through the same processes, but the time taken on each process varies as shown:-

	A Process hours per unit	B Process hours per unit	Total process hours available
Process 1	2	6	66
Process 2	8	4	120
Process 3	4	8	96

The expected profit on style A is £16, and style B is £12.

How many of style A and style B should be produced to give maximum profit?

4. Two products I and II are produced by a firm, each of which pass through three separate processes during manufacture. The details of the time spent in each process with the available capacity is given in the following table:

	Cutting	Welding	Finishing
Product I	1 hour	5 hours	3 hours
Product II	2 hours	4 hours	1 hour
Available capacity	720 hours	1,800 hours	900 hours

Profit for each product is £80 for I and £100 for II. Find by the Simplex Method the optimum product mix for the period being considered. State how much spare capacity is available from your solution.

SOLUTIONS TO EXERCISES

1. Let x be the number of type I shelving.
   Let y be the number of type II shelving.

Sheet Metal	=	20x + 30y	≤	2,400
Sheet Rodding	=	30xx+ 30y	≤	2,700
Labour	=	6x + 4y	≤	480
Minimum production	=	x	=	40

   Objective function: Maximum Profit = 3x + 3.6y.

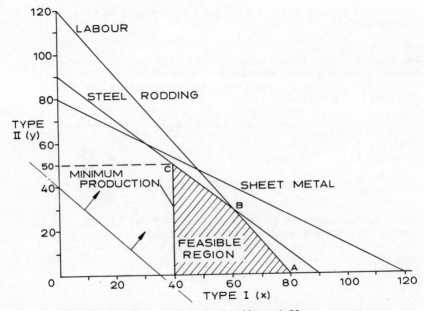

   Maximum Profit at point C = 40x and 50y
                             = 40 x 3 + 50 x 3.6
                             = £300.

   Produce 40 units of Type I
   Produce 50 units of Type II.

2. The conversion of capacity requirements to units of production is as follows:

	Shaping	Setting	Finishing
Type A	1,000	600	1,200
Type B	900	900	450

Objective function = $10A + 12\frac{1}{2}B$ = MAX

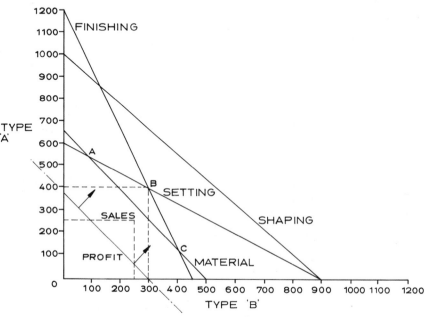

(a) At point 'b' where Type A reads 400 and Type B reads 300, which gives a profit of $400 \times 10 + 300 \times 12\frac{1}{2} = £7,750$.

(b) Any agreed mix would be satisfactory along the line A - C of the materials concerned.

(c) Manufacture to meet sales demand, as the other constraints do not now apply.

3. Let the number of style A produced = x.
   Let the number of style B produced = y.

Constraints:

Process I	$2x + 6y$	$\leq$	66
2	$8x + 4y$	$\leq$	120
3	$4x + 8y$	$\leq$	96

Objective function = $16x + 12y$ = MAX

Equations to equalities:

$$2x + 6y + S_1 \qquad\qquad = 66$$
$$8x + 4y \quad + S_2 \qquad = 120$$
$$4x + 8y \qquad + S_3 = 96$$

Objective function = $16x + 12y + 0S_1 + 0S_2 + 0S_3$

First Matrix

			16	12	0	0	0	
			x	y	S_1	S_2	S_3	
0	S_1	66	2	6	1	0	0	
0	S_2	120	[8]	4	0	1	0	◄— PIVOT ROW
0	S_3	96	4	8	0	0	1	
			-16	-12	0	0	0	

PIVOT
COLUMN

Second Matrix

				16	12	0	0	0	
				x	y	S_1	S_2	S_3	
0	0	S_1	36	0	5	1	$\frac{1}{4}$	0	
	16	x	15	1	$\frac{1}{2}$	0	$\frac{1}{8}$	0	
	0	S_3	36	0	[6]	0	$\frac{1}{2}$	1	◄— PIVOT ROW
				0	-8	0	2	0	

PIVOT
COLUMN

Third Matrix

			16	12	0	0	0
			x	y	S_1	S_2	S_3
0	S_1	6	0	0	1	$\frac{1}{6}$	$\frac{5}{6}$
16	x	12	1	0	0	$\frac{1}{12}$	$\frac{1}{12}$
12	y	6	0	1	0	$-\frac{1}{12}$	$\frac{1}{6}$
		264	0	0	0	$\frac{4}{12}$	$\frac{8}{12}$

Solution: produce 12 of style A
produce 6 of style B

Expected profit $(12 \times 16) + (6 \times 12)$ = £264

4. Let x be the amount of product I
Let y be the amount of product II

Constraints:

Cutting	=	x + 2y	$\leqq$	720
Welding	=	5x + 4y	$\leqq$	1,800
Finishing	=	3x + y	$\leqq$	900

Objective function = $80x + 100y$ = MAX

Equations to equalities

$x + 2y + S_1 = 720$
$5x + 4y + S_2 = 1,800$
$3x + y + S_3 = 900$

Objective function = $80x + 100y + 0S_1 + 0S_2 + 0S_3$

First Matrix

			80	100	0	0	0	
			x	y	S_1	S_2	S_3	
0	S_1	720	1	2	1	0	0	◄—PIVOT ROW
0	S_2	1,800	5	4	0	1	0	
0	S_3	900	3	1	0	0	1	
		0	-80	-100	0	0	0	

PIVOT
COLUMN

Second Matrix

			80 x	100 y	0 S_1	0 S_2	0 S_3	
100	y	360	$\frac{1}{2}$	1	$\frac{1}{2}$	0	0	
0	S_2	360	$\boxed{3}$	0	-2	1	0	←PIVOT ROW
0	S_3	540	$\frac{5}{2}$	0	$\frac{1}{2}$	0	1	
		36,000	-30	0	50	0	0	

PIVOT
COLUMN

Third Matrix

			80 x	100 y	0 S_1	0 S_2	0 S_3
80	y	300	0	1	$\frac{1}{6}$	$\frac{1}{6}$	0
100	x	120	1	0	$-\frac{2}{3}$	$\frac{1}{3}$	0
0	S_3	240	0	0	$\frac{4}{3}$	$-\frac{5}{2}$	1
		39,600	0	0	30	10	0

Solution: produce 120 of product I
produce 300 of product II

240 hours idle in the finishing department.

Profit = 120 x 80 + 300 x 100 = £39,600

Application

1. HOUSEHOLD PRODUCTS

For many years a rigid policy on advertising had been adopted by Household Products due mainly to the influence of the marketing manager. Since his retirement a more flexible approach had gradually emerged and with new management recently appointed it was anticipated this flexibility would increase.

The company's main products were always advertised in two particular magazines and the same number of insertions or runs were made. An agreed sum of money was allocated each year for advertising and budgets made for individual products.

In the coming year a decision has been made to allocate £120,000 for an advertising programme on one of the products. The advertising programme to consist of running two different advertisements in the magazines usually adopted. Recent negotiations on costs with the magazine owners confirmed that Magazine 1 would charge £2,000 per run and Magazine 2 £5,000 per run.

Previous experience had shown that at least ten runs were necessary in Magazine 2 and at least 20 runs in Magazine 1 were necessary to make any appreciable penetration to the market. Experience also indicates that there is no reason to make more than 50 total in both magazines.

The management team wished to consider alternative policies that could be adopted if necessary but doubted whether the information available was sufficient for this to be possible.

The problem was given to the management services section for consideration. It was requested that if possible a full report be presented showing the various possible polcies that management could adopt.

Is there sufficient data to meet the request? Also would it be possible to state how many runs should be made in Magazine 1 and how many in Magazine 2 to satisfy the restrictions and still not exceed the £120,000 budget?

Discussion

What would be the effect if the decision to increase the advertising budget to £200,000 was made and the number of runs on the two magazines was 25 for Magazine 1 and 12 for Magazine 2. New costs for the runs were now to be £2,500 for Magazine 1 and the £5,000 cost for Magazine 2 could be maintained.

2. GUY'S FIREWORKS LIMITED

Guy's Fireworks Limited was a progressive company manufacturing special types of fireworks, mainly for export. The company had concentrated on the safety aspect of fireworks, incorporating many features such as handles and length of fuse to assist in the reduction of accidents.

Special blending of the ingredients plus the safety aspects and competitive nature of the product, made the fireworks very popular particularly in the Middle Eastern countries.

Three main types of firework are produced: Highlight, Twinlight and Crimson Flash. Each type contains three basic ingredients; sulphur potassium nitrate and carbon, plus a certain inert ingredient. The mixture is made in large tanks and fed to an assembly line where the fireworks are completed.

The following table shows the mix used to make the three types of firework and the cost per ton:

Percentage mix (by weight)

Type	Sulphur	Potassium Nitrate	Carbon	Inert Ingredient
Highlight	5	10	5	80
Twinlight	5	10	10	75
Crimson Flash	10	10	10	70
Cost per ton (£)	160	40	100	5

The cost of mixing, packaging and selling the fireworks, which is based on a tonnage basis, is £15.

Because of the competition in selling fireworks, particularly from the Far East, the company has to sell at the following prices:

Highlight	£40 per ton
Twinlight	£50 per ton
Crimson Flash	£60 per ton

Each month the company plans production for the following month and on this particular occasion they will have available, either in stock or guaranteed delivery: 1,000 tons sulphur; 1,800 tons potassium nitrate and 12,000 tons carbon. No further supplies will be available in the coming month.

The company wishes to mix the ingredients, together with the inert ingredient, of which there is unlimited supply, to give the maximum profit in the month to come.

The three types of firework being considered can be sold at the figures given in the coming month, but there is a sales commitment to deliver 6,000 tons of Highlight within the month.

What should the production planning schedule be to give maximum profit?

Discussion

If, because of competition, the selling price per ton of the three types of firework was reduced to: Highlight, no change; Twinlight, £45 per ton and Crimson Flash, £50 per ton, would you alter your production schedule to give greater profit?

3. THE ORIENT FASHION COMPANY

The Orient Fashion Company, who specialise in the manufacture of cloth, was renowned for its quality and reasonable cost of the finished product. The designs were based on the oriental style and were becoming very popular in the European markets.

Although the company produced many different designs, in the last two years eight particular styles had become popular sellers and were known in the trade as 'The Top 8".

In the past two years the company's profits on 'The Top 8' had decreased and it was agreed that the recently created Operational Research Department would look at this particular problem and report their findings. Putting forward recommendations on which style mix would give the maximum total contribution to profits and overheads was to be part of the brief given to the O.R. Department.

It was found that the head of sales selected styles for production, a man of vast experience in the trade who also set prices for each style,which had always resulted in the company being able to sell all 'The Top 8' it could produce.

After a careful study of the pricing system it was found that the prices charged for each style was satisfactory and methods of production were also satisfactory. It was agreed that an exercise be carried out to see if any particular style would give a greater contribution to profits than another. Should it be found that this was the case, production schedules could be modified to take advantage of this, as the problem of selling such styles would be minimal.

There were several constraints within which the problem had to be solved. The company had a three shift system, each of 40 hours' duration. The cloth had four production processes, these being carding, drawing, spinning and weaving.

The contribution to profit and overheads for the style at the prices being charged are shown in Table I.

Table I
Contribution to Profit and Overheads for 'The Top 8'
in £s per 100,000 yards

Style		Contribution (£)
Asian	(A)	400
Chine	(C)	370
Fiji	(F)	360
Indo	(I)	360
Korean	(K)	350
Malay	(M)	330
Nippon	(N)	280
Thai	(T)	275

160

Having obtained this information, the total available time for the four processes which all cloth had to receive was as shown in Table II. These figures were for a 120 hour (three shifts) week.

TABLE II

Process	Available time (in thousands of hours)
Carding	26.0
Drawing	242.0
Spinning	7,200.0
Weaving	250.0

Because of the variation in design and finish, the production hours required for each style varied and these are found in Table III:

TABLE III
Thousands of production hours per 100,000 yards

Style		Carding	Drawing	Spinning	Weaving
Asian	(A)	1.8	36.0	720.0	30.6
Chine	(C)	2.6.	28.8	648.0	30.6
Fiji	(F)	2.4	28.8	720.0	32.6
Indo	(I)	2.1	28.8	648.0	30.6
Korean	(K)	2.9	31.2	648.0	26.5
Malay	(M)	2.1	36.0	720.0	30.6
Nippon	(N)	2.9	21.6	792.0	22.4
Thai	(T)	2.9	36.0	720.0	32.8

Discussion

An associate company was asking for assistance in the way of capacity that may be available particularly in carding and weaving. The request was for 9,000 hours of both operations and the Operations Research Department was asked to investigate the possibility of these hours being available within the present restrictions. What conclusions can be obtained from the solution?

Because of employment problems in skilled labour not being available in the district, it was envisaged that a two shift system would be operated in the coming year. A further study of the problem was considered necessary so that this restriction could be considered. What effect, if any, would it have?

Contribution to profits and overheads was expected to fall within the next two years which, for technical reasons, would affect the Asian and Chine style to the extent of reducing the present figures by 10%per cent. Would this have any effect on the present solution?

161

Solutions to applications

1. HOUSEHOLD PRODUCTS

Let X equal the number of runs in Magazine 1.
Let Y equal the number of runs in Magazine 2.

The total cost of all runs is to be equal to or less than £120,000.

£2,000 + £5,000 $\leq$ £120,000

This is the total cost equation. The equations for the restrictions
are:

X = 20   for the number of runs in Magazine 1

Y = 10   for the number of runs in Magazine 2

also,

X + Y = 50   for the total number of runs.

Figure 1. shows the cost equation and the three restrictions plotted.
Only the shaded triangle contains feasible values of X and Y, that is,
the values which will satisfy all three restrictions.

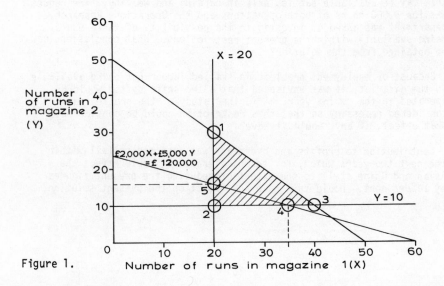

Figure 1.

We only consider the shaded area and perimeters. It is only necessary to check out the values of X and Y at the vertices 1, 2 and 3 of the triangle.

Consider Vertex 1:

The X and Y values of vertex 1 substituted into the cost equation yield:

$$£2,000 \times 20 + £5,000 \times 30 = £190,000$$

This is greater than the £120,000 budget and therefore not optimal. However, this vertex does maximise the number of runs in Magazine 2, while satisfying all the restrictions.

Consider Vertex 2:

This yields:

$$£2,000 \times 20 + £5,000 \times 10 = £90,000$$

This solution would be acceptable, which would leave a surplus of £30,000 from the original budget of £120,000. This vertex gives the LEAST expensive solution to the problem.

Consider Vertex 3:

This yields:

$$£2,000 \times 40 + £5,000 \times 10 = £130,000$$

This gives an additional £10,000 in the advertising budget, spent optimally, will buy a further 20 runs in the least expensive magazine, Magazine 1. This vertex maximises the number of runs in Magazine 1, while satisfying all the restrictions.

Alternatives

If the manager wishes to spend EXACTLY £120,000, then any solutions along the cost line from vertex 5 to 4 are acceptable. That is, the solutions range from 20 runs in Magazine 1, plus 16 runs in Magazine 2, to 35 runs in Magazine 1 plus 10 runs in Magazine 2.

The ultimate choice of an optimum policy will thus depend upon the importance which the company gives to the number of runs in each magazine and the flexibility of the budget.

2. GUY'S FIREWORKS LIMITED

In the model let

Highlight	=	X_1
Twinlight	=	X_2
Crimson Flash	=	X_3
Sulphur	=	S_1
Potassium nitrate	=	S_2
Carbon	=	S_3
Inert ingredient	=	S_4

The company has a sales commitment of 6,000 Highlight (X_1), therefore the ingredient requirements are:

5%	of S_1	x 6,000	=	300 tons
10%	of S_2	x 6,000	=	600 tons
5%	of S_3	x 6,000	=	300 tons
80%	of S_4	x 6,000	= 4,800 tons

	Tonnage Available	Tonnage Committed (X_1)	Tonnage Uncommitted
S_1	1,000	300	700
S_2	1,800	600	1,200
S_3	12,000	300	11,700
S_4	$\propto$	4,800	$\propto$
		Total 6,000	

Costs involved:

Highlight (X_1)		Twinlight (X_2)		Crimson Flash (X_3)	
5% of £160	= £ 8.00	5% of £160	= £ 8.00	10% of £160	= £16.00
10% of £ 40	= £ 4.00	10% of £ 40	= £ 4.00	10% of £ 40	= £ 4.00
5% of £100	= £ 5.00	10% of £100	= £10.00	10% of £100	= £10.00
80% of £ 5	= £ 4.00	75% of £ 5	= £ 3.75	70% of £ 5	= £ 3.50
	£21.00		£25.75		£33.50
Fixed costs	£15.00		£15.00		£15.00
	£36.00		£40.75		£48.50
Selling price	£40.00		£50.00		£60.00
Profit Contribution	£ 4.00		£ 9.25		£11.50

MODEL

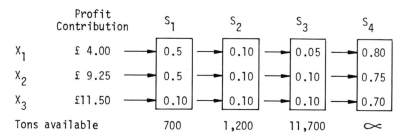

	Profit Contribution	S_1	S_2	S_3	S_4
X_1	£ 4.00	0.5	0.10	0.05	0.80
X_2	£ 9.25	0.5	0.10	0.10	0.75
X_3	£11.50	0.10	0.10	0.10	0.70
Tons available		700	1,200	11,700	∞

MODEL FOR SIMPLEX

$0.05X_1 + 0.05X_2 + 0.10X_3 + 1S_1 + 0S_2 + 0S_3 + 0S_4 = 700$

$0.10X_1 + 0.10X_2 + 0.10X_3 + 0S_1 + 1S_2 + 0S_3 + 0S_4 = 1,200$

$0.05X_1 + 0.10X_2 + 0.10X_3 + 0S_1 + 0S_2 + 1S_3 + 0S_4 = 11,700$

$0.80X_1 + 0.75X_2 + 0.70X_3 + 0S_1 + 0S_2 + 0S_3 + 1S_4 = \infty$

165

GUY'S FIREWORKS LIMITED

Table 1
Initial Solution

	Mix	Quantity	4.00 X_1	9.25 X_2	11.50 X_3	0 S_1	0 S_2	0 S_3	0 S_4	
0	S_1	700	0.05	0.05	0.10	1	0	0	1	→ PIVOT ROW
0	S_2	1,200	0.10	0.10	0.10	0	1	0	0	
0	S_3	11,700	0.05	0.10	0.10	0	0	1	0	
0	S_4	∞	0.80	0.75	0.70	0	0	0	1	
		0	-4.00	-9.25	-11.50	0	0	0	0	

PIVOT COLUMN

$$\frac{\infty}{0.70} = \infty$$

$$\frac{11,700}{0.10} = 117,000$$

$$\frac{1,200}{0.10} = 12,000$$

$$\frac{700}{0.10} = 7,000 \quad \text{LIMITING FACTOR}$$

166

Table 2

		4.00	9.25	11.50	0	0	0	0	
Mix	Quantity	X_1	X_2	X_3	S_1	S_2	S_3	S_4	
11.50 X_3	7,000	0.5	0.5	1	10	0	0	0	
0 S_2	500	0.05	0.05	0	-1	1	0	0	⟵ PIVOT ROW
0 S_3	11,000	0	0.05	0	-1	0	1	0	
0 S_4	∞	0.45	0.40	0	-7	0	0	1	
		1.75	-3.5	0	115	0	0	0	

PIVOT COLUMN

$$\frac{7,000}{0.5} = 14,000$$

$$\frac{500}{0.05} = 10,000 \quad \text{LIMITING FACTOR}$$

$$\frac{11,000}{0.05} = 220,000$$

$$\frac{∞}{0.40} = ∞$$

167

Table 3

	Mix	Quantity	X_1	X_2	X_3	S_1	S_2	S_3	S_4
11.50	X_3	2,000	0	0	1	20	-10	0	0
9.25	X_2	10,000	1	1	0	-20	20	0	0
0	S_3	10,500	-0.05	0	0	0	-1	1	0
0	S_4	∞	0.05	0	0	1	8	0	1
			5.25	0	0	45	70	0	0

(sales commitment)

Conclusion:

Produce	6,000	X_1	@ £4.00	contribution	=	£24,000	
Produce	10,000	X_2	@ £9.25	contribution	=	£92,500	
Produce	2,000	X_3	@ £11.50	contribution	=	£23,000	
				Total		£139,500	

3. ORIENT FASHION COMPANY

Constraints

1. $1.8A + 2.6C + 2.4F + 2.1I + 2.9K + 2.1M + 2.9N + 2.9T$
   $+ 0S_1 + 0S_2 + 0S_3 + 0S_4$ - Carding constraint.

2. $36.0A + 28.8C + 28.8F + 28.8I + 31.2K + 36.0M + 21.6N + 36.0T$
   $+ 0S_1 + 0S_2 + 0S_3 + 0S_4$ - Drawing constraint.

3. $720A + 648C + 720F + 648I + 648K + 720M + 792N + 720T$
   $+ 0S_1 + 0S_2 + 0S_3 + 0S_4$ - Spinning constraint.

4. $30.6A + 30.6C + 32.6F + 30.6I + 26.5K + 30.6M + 22.4N + 32.8T$
   $+ 0S_1 + 0S_2 + 0S_3 + 0S_4$ - Weaving constraint.

Objective function

$400A + 370C + 360F + 360I + 350K + 330M + 280N + 275T$ = Maximum

ORIENT FASHION COMPANY

Table 1
Initial Solution

Cont.	Mix	Quantity	A 400	C 370	F 360	I 360	K 350	M 330	N 280	T 275	S₁ 0	S₂ 0	S₃ 0	S₄ 0
0	S_1	26	1.8	2.6	2.4	2.1	2.9	2.1	2.9	2.9	1	0	0	0
0	S_2	242	[36]	28.8	28.8	28.8	31.2	36.0	21.6	36.0	0	1	0	0
0	S_3	7,200	720	648	720	648	648	720	792	720	0	0	1	0
0	S_4	250	30.6	30.6	32.6	30.6	26.5	30.6	22.4	32.8	0	0	0	1
		0	-400	-370	-360	-360	-350	-330	-280	-275	0	0	0	0

PIVOT COLUMN

PIVOT ROW

LIMITING FACTOR

$$\frac{26}{1.8} = 14.4$$

$$\frac{242}{36} = 6.72$$

$$\frac{7,200}{720} = 10$$

$$\frac{250}{30.6} = 8.16$$

170

Table 2
Introducing Variable A

Cont.	Mix	Quantity	400 A	370 C	360 F	360 I	350 K	330 M	280 N	275 T	0 S_1	0 S_2	0 S_3	0 S_4
0	S_1	13.9	0	1.16	1	0.66	1.34	0.3	1.8	1.1	1	-0.05	0	0
400	A	6.72	1	0.8	0.8	0.8	.86	1	0.6	1	0	0.03	0	0
0	S_3	2,360	0	72	144	72	24	0	360	0	0	-20	1	0
0	S_4	44	0	[6.1]	8.1	6.1	0	0	4	2.2	0	-0.85	0	1 ← PIVOT ROW
		2,689	0	-50	-40	-40	-3	70	-40	125	0	-11.1	0	0

PIVOT COLUMN

$$\frac{13.9}{1.16} = 11.98$$

$$\frac{6.72}{0.8} = 8.4$$

$$\frac{2,360}{72} = 32.77$$

$$\frac{44}{6.1} = 7.2 \quad \text{LIMITING FACTOR}$$

171

Table 3
Introducing Variable C

Cont.	Mix	Quantity	400 A	370 C	360 F	360 I	350 K	330 M	280 N	275 T	0 S_1	0 S_2	0 S_3	0 S_4	
0	S_1	5.54	0	0	-0.54	-0.5	1.34	0.3	1.04	0.7	1	0.1	0	-0.19	← PIVOT ROW
400	A	0.95	1	0	-0.26	0	0.86	1	0.08	0.72	0	0.14	0	-0.16	
0	S_3	1,841	0	0	48.4	0	24	0	313	-25.9	0	-10	1	-11.8	
370	C	7.2	0	1	1.32	1	0	0	.11	.36	0	-0.14	0	0.17	
		3,050	0	0	26.4	10	-3	70	-7	143	0	-18	0	8.2	

PIVOT COLUMN → (under N)   LIMITING FACTOR

$$\frac{5.54}{1.04} = 5.32$$

$$\frac{0.95}{0.08} = 11.8$$

$$\frac{1,841}{313} = 5.88$$

$$\frac{7.2}{0.11} = 65.4$$

Table 4
Introducing Variable N

Cont.	Mix	Quantity	400 A	370 C	360 F	360 I	350 K	330 M	280 N	275 T	0 S$_1$	0 S$_2$	0 S$_3$	0 S$_4$
280	N	5.32	0	0	-0.52	0.48	1.29	0.28	1	0.67	0.96	0.1	0	0.18
400	A	0.52	1	0	-0.22	0.03	0.76	.98	0	0.67	-0.07	0.14	0	-0.15
0	S$_3$	174	0	0	211	150	-379	223	0	-237	-301	-40	1	45.2
370	C	6.6	0	1	1.37	0.95	-0.14	.03	0	0.29	-0.1	-0.15	0	0.19
			0	0	22.7	6.6	6	72	0	147.7	6.73	-17.3	0	6.9

The optimum solution is to produce:

532,000 yards of Nippon.	Profit	=	5.32	×	£280	=	£1,490
52,000 yards of Asian.	Profit	=	0.52	×	£400	=	£ 208
660,000 yards of Chine.	Profit	=	6.60	×	£370	=	£2,442
						Total	£4,140

7 Forecasting

In reviewing a copy of an English dictionary the word 'forecast' is defined as 'conjecture' and 'guess at future event'. In defining 'conjecture' it states 'guesswork', 'summise'. From this one would conclude that a forecast must by definition be based on insufficient evidence.

By collecting and analysing data from the past we project into the future. Rarely are all the facts relating to past forecasting errors known and all forecasts are wrong to some degree. With this fact in mind forecasters are still expected to be exact in their predictions!

The method of making forecasts depends not only on the inputs available in terms of data, manpower and time, but also on the output required in terms of accuracy and for how far ahead the forecast is required. It is often possible to increase the accuracy of forecasting with increased cost in time and money, the expenditure of which can only be justified if the increased accuracy gives the desired benefits.

Although 'accurate' forecasting can be a difficult process for two main reasons we must make 'predictions', which is to foretell or prophesy.

1. Any reasoned calculation is better than guessing.

2. Forecasting is a learning process.

Although almost every forecasting problem is unique, there are techniques or methods which can assist us.

CLASSIFICATION OF FORECASTS

Two generally accepted areas of study in forecasting can be classified as follows:

1. Short-term forecasting

   This is generally for the period 1 - 6 months ahead and is closely tied to current operations in areas such as budgetting, production scheduling, and where sales and raw material operations can be completed in this period.

2. Long-term forecasting

   Forecasts in this classification are usually required for decisions about activities that will continue for a year or more ahead and concern events that will necessitate changes in the use of existing facilities. Examples of this could be financial planning, changes in product range, sales and advertising campaigns.

METHODS OF FORECASTING

Although a variety of methods are used in practice they are not always applicable to the problem under study. Two main study areas can be considered.

1. Synthetic forecasts

   These are made from reports received from customers, sales force or individuals and have the advantage of using the direct information. The big disadvantage is the problem of bias and inadequate coverage.

2. Analytical forecasts

   Here the data is broken down into trends (T), which gives the general direction in which the data appears to be going over a period of time. Any seasonal movements (S) or variations are studied, which refer to identical, or almost identical, patterns which appear to follow corresponding months of successive years.

   Finally, any irregular or random movements (I) are observed. By studying the effect of the three areas, TREND (T), SEASONAL (S) and IRREGULAR (I), it may be possible to reassemble the individual elements and make a future projection. This is called TIME SERIES ANALYSIS.

   To build a forecasting model based on time series analyses we assume that the time series variable X is a product of the variables T, S and I. For many forecasting problems the model is acceptable in this form.

   $$T \times S \times I = X \qquad \underline{\qquad}(1)$$

   or

   $$T + S + I = X \qquad \underline{\qquad}(2)$$

Whichever model is used depends on the degree of success in applying the assumption.

Moving averages

From equation (2) the variable X, which we will assume refers to monthly sales, can be re-written:

$$S + I = X - T \qquad \underline{\qquad}(3)$$

If we could calculate the trend of sales, we could obtain the net sum of seasonal and irregular fluctuations by deducting the trend from the actual monthly sales. A method of obtaining the trend is by moving averages.

EXAMPLE 1.

The following Table 7.1. gives the sales of goods over a five year period. Plot the data and show the trend of monthly sales using the method of moving averages.

Table 7.1.
Table of sales for five years

Monthly Sales Company A 1974-78 (in £s)

Month	1974	1975	1976	1977	1978
January	12	13	15	19	20
February	11	14	17	20	21
March	12	13	15	18	20
April	11	12	14	16	19
May	11	11	12	14	17
June	10	9	11	13	16
July	10	10	11	14	18
August	11	11	13	15	21
September	11	12	15	16	22
October	12	12	16	17	23
November	13	13	16	18	23
December	13	14	17	19	24
	137	144	172	199	244

The calculation of the averages of the twelve monthly cycles from January to December are given in Table 7.2, column 2. They are calculated by progressively adding the current year's monthly sales and dividing by twelve, e.g. to obtain the moving twelve monthly total for January 1975 would involve:

Yearly total 1974 - January figure 1978 + January figure 1975

hence   137   -   12   +   13   = 138

dividing this by 12 gives the moving monthly average: $\frac{138}{12}$ = 11.5

The calculation for February 1975 would be:

138 - 11 + 14 = 141

moving monthly average = $\frac{141}{12}$ = 11.7 and so on.

176

Table 7.2.
Moving average of sales

Month	1974		1975		1976		1977		1978	
	Moving 12 month total (1)	Moving monthly average (2)	(1)	(2)	(1)	(2)	(1)	(2)	(1)	(2)
January			138	11.5	146	12.2	176	14.6	200	16.7
February			141	11.7	149	12.4	179	14.9	201	16.7
March			142	11.8	151	12.6	182	15.1	203	16.9
April			143	11.9	153	12.7	184	15.3	206	17.1
May			143	11.9	154	12.8	186	15.5	209	17.4
June			142	11.8	156	13.0	188	15.7	212	17.6
July			142	11.8	157	13.1	191	15.9	216	18.0
August			142	11.8	159	13.2	193	16.1	222	18.5
September			143	11.9	162	13.5	194	16.2	228	19.0
October			143	11.9	166	13.8	195	16.2	234	19.5
November			143	11.9	169	14.1	197	16.4	239	19.9
December	137	11.4	144	12.0	172	14.3	199	16.6	244	20.3

The monthly moving averages are plotted at the mid-point of each year over which the average has been computed and is shown as a dashed line on Figure 7.1. The curve arising from these points is the line of trend. One disadvantage of this method is that the line terminates 'early', which in this case is at June 1978. To continue beyond this period requires 1979 data or extended freehand and later confirmed when data becomes available.

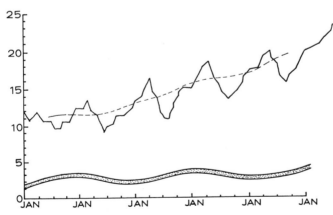

Figure 7.1. Graph showing trend of monthly sales.

Having obtained the trend and plotted it as shown in Figure 7.1. we can review the equation (3). The difference between the continuous and dashed line will give us the fluctuations caused by the seasonal and irregular factors S and I.

Seasonal and Irregular variation

We can extend the problem and carry out further analysis to obtain the seasonal and other irregular variations as shown in Table 7.3. From Table 7.2, column (2) we can obtain a figure for the trend but this is 'centred' by averaging two successive months at a time, e.g. January 1975 = 11.5 and February 1975 = 11.7, these average at 11.6 and will coincide with August 1974, and so on for successive months. These calculations are shown in Table 7.3, column (3). By subtracting the trend (T) from the actual monthly sales (X) we have the total remaining fluctuation which is entered in column (4), Table 7.3.

To obtain the seasonal variation, the averaging of the deviation from the trend for each month is calculated to form Table 7.4. These figures obtained are then entered in Table 7.3, column (5). By subtracting column (5) from column (4) the total variation remaining is calculated and shown in column (6).

In reviewing column (6) the variations having comparative high or low values would warrant investigation.

Freehand method of curve fitting

As already mentioned, individual judgement can be used to draw the trend through plotted data. If the equation of the curve is known, it is possible to obtain the constants in the equation by choosing as many points on the curve as there are constants in the equation. If the curve is a straight line only two points are necessary if a parabola then three are required.

The method, however, is not recommended because individual judgement can vary considerably. One method used to obtain a line of 'best fit' through data, which eliminates any individual variation obtained by freehand drawing is 'Method of Least Squares'.

The Method of Least Squares

The simplest type of approximating curve is a straight line, whose equation can be written $y = mx + c$, where x is usually considered the independent variable and y the dependent; m is called the slope of the line and represents the change in y divided by the corresponding change in x and is a constant; c denotes the value of y when $x = 0$ and is called the y intercept, also a constant value. A straight line based on this equation is drawn through the original data and the test of whether the line is a 'best fit', is whether the sum of squares of the distances between successive points on the curve and original data is minimised, hence the name of the method.

178

Table 7.3.
Monthly variation of sales

Month	Sales Monthly	Trend (T)	Fluctuation from trend (2) - (3)	Seasonal Variation	Residual Variation (4) - (5)
(1)	(2)	(3)	(4)	(5)	(6)
1974 July	10	11.4	-1.4	-2.4	+1.0
August	11	11.6	-0.6	-1.3	+0.7
September	11	11.7	-0.7	-0.5	-0.2
October	12	11.8	+0.2	+0.1	+0.1
November	13	11.9	+1.1	+0.7	+0.4
December	13	11.9	+1.1	+1.3	-0.2
1975 January	13	11.8	+1.2	+2.1	-0.9
February	14	11.8	+2.2	+3.2	-1.0
March	13	11.8	+1.2	+1.5	-0.3
April	12	11.9	+0.1	+0.02	+0.08
May	11	11.9	-0.9	-1.9	+1.0
June	9	11.9	-2.9	-3.4	+0.5
July	10	12.1	-2.1	-2.4	+0.3
August	11	12.3	-1.3	-1.3	0
September	12	12.5	-0.5	-0.5	0
October	12	12.6	-0.6	+0.1	-0.7
November	13	12.7	+0.3	+0.7	-0.4
December	14	12.9	+1.1	+1.3	-0.2
1976 January	15	13.0	+2.0	+ 2.1	-0.1
February	17	13.1	+3.9	+3.2	+0.7
March	15	13.3	+1.7	+1.5	+0.2
April	14	13.6	+0.4	+0.02	+0.38
May	12	13.9	-1.9	-1.9	0
June	11	14.2	-3.2	-3.4	+0.2
July	11	14.4	-3.4	-2.4	-1.0
August	13	14.7	-1.7	-1.3	-0.4
September	15	15.0	0	-0.5	+0.5
October	16	15.2	+0.8	+0.1	+0.7
November	16	15.4	+0.6	+0.7	-0.1
December	17	15.6	+1.4	+1.3	+0.1
1977 January	19	15.8	+3.2	+2.1	+1.1
February	20	16.0	+4.0	+3.2	+0.8
March	18	16.1	+1.9	+1.5	+0.4
April	16	16.2	-0.2	+0.02	-0.22
May	14	16.3	-2.3	-1.9	-0.4
June	13	16.5	-3.5	-3.4	-0.1
July	14	16.6	-2.6	-2.4	-0.2
August	15	16.7	-1.7	-1.3	-0.4
September	16	16.8	-0.8	-0.5	-0.3
October	17	17.0	0	+0.1	-0.1
November	18	17.2	+0.8	+0.7	+0.1
December	19	17.5	+1.5	+1.3	+0.2
1978 January	20	17.8	+2.2	+2.1	+0.1
February	21	18.2	+2.8	+3.2	-0.4
March	20	18.7	+1.3	+1.5	-0.2
April	19	19.2	-0.2	+0.02	-0.22
May	17	19.7	-2.7	-1.9	-0.8
June	16	20.1	-4.1	-3.4	-0.7

Table 7.4.
Seasonal variation analysis

Year	Months											
	Jan	Feb	Mar	Apr	May	June	July	Aug	Sept	Oct	Nov	Dec
1974							-1.4	-0.6	-0.7	+0.2	+1.1	+1.1
1975	+1.2	+2.2	+1.2	+0.1	-0.9	-2.9	-2.1	-1.3	-0.5	-0.6	+0.3	+1.1
1976	+2.0	+3.9	+1.7	+0.4	-1.9	-3.2	-3.4	-1.7	0	+0.8	+0.6	+1.4
1977	+3.2	+4.0	+1.9	-0.2	-2.3	-3.5	-2.6	-1.7	-0.8	0	+0.8	+1.5
1978	+2.2	+2.8	+1.3	-0.2	-2.7	-4.1						
Total	+8.6	+12.9	+6.1	+0.1	-7.8	-13.7	-9.5	-5.3	-2.0	+0.4	+2.8	+5.1
Seasonal Varia-tion	+2.1	+3.2	+1.5	+0.02	-1.9	-3.4	-2.4	-1.3	-0.5	+0.1	+0.7	+1.3

The equations which represent the best fit of this straight line to a group of data (x, y) are as follows,

$$\sum y = cn + m \sum x \qquad \text{_____(4)}$$
$$\sum xy = c \sum x + m \sum x^2 \qquad \text{_____(5)}$$

where n is the number of periods or items being considered. For most business purposes the method of least squares is acceptable, where problems involving two variables are subject to the analysis.

Further extending the previous problem which enables us to use existing data, a trend through the data is required using the method of least squares. Half yearly periods have been used in this example, January - June and July - December, these are shown in Table 7.5, column (1). The periods are numbered 1-10, column (2), and the sales for each half yearly period entered in column (3).

From Table 7.5. the four totals necessary for substitution in equations (4) and (5) are:

$$\sum x = 55 \quad \sum y = 896$$
$$\sum xy = 5,478 \quad \sum x^2 = 385$$

$$896 = 10c + 55m \qquad \text{_____(4)}$$
$$5,478 = 55c + 385m \qquad \text{_____(5)}$$

These are simultaneous equations in c and m. Multiplying through (4) by 5.5 we obtain:

$$4,928 = 55c + 302.5m$$
$$5,478 = 55c + 385.0m$$

hence   550   =   82.5m

thus   m   =   6.66

substituting m in either equation (4) or (5),   c = 53.

Table 7.5.

Half year (1)	Period x (2)	Total sales y (3)	Σxy (4)	x^2 (5)
Jan - June 1974	1	67	67	1
July - Dec 1974	2	70	140	4
Jan - June 1975	3	72	216	9
July - Dec 1975	4	72	288	16
Jan - June 1976	5	84	420	25
July - Dec 1976	6	88	528	36
Jan - June 1977	7	100	700	49
July - Dec 1977	8	99	792	64
Jan - June 1978	9	113	1,017	81
July - Dec 1978	10	131	1,310	100
Totals	55	896	5,478	385

The equation to the straight line which represents the trend of sales for the period 1974-78 is:

$y = 6.66x + 53.$

Thus for any period x the value of sales y can be obtained from the equation.

The line of 'best fit' through the plotted sales figures for the half yearly totals is shown in Figure 7.2.

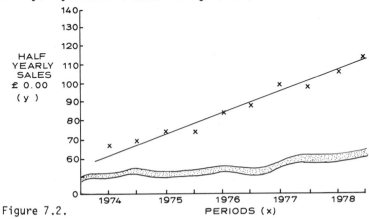

Figure 7.2.

When the trend line is drawn against the plotted data, the
variation between them for each period can be measured by observing
the vertical distances between the point on the trend line and
plotted data.

Limitation of techniques

Using the 'method of least squares' enables us to fit a line through
the data and when a single forecast is required it is a very useful
method. However, there are many problems that involve the necessity
to have the forecast updated on a day to day basis. The least squares
method is limited in this type of problem and therefore we require
a method that is adaptive, i.e. one that is easy to revise and correct
for the difference between actual data and the forecast.

The moving average is adaptive but the data at the beginning and
end of the series is lost. A further disadvantage is that the moving
average may generate cycles or other movements which were not
present in the original data and are affected by extreme values.

With the moving average we give equal weighting to all the data and
we could argue that the latest data should have a greater influence
than the older data on the final figure. With this in mind the
following method can be adopted.

Weighted averages

A more sophisticated way of including more items in a moving average
whilst allowing for the unrealiability of including too many of the
older figures is to adopt a system of 'weighting' the average. In
this method a fixed series of numbers, called weights, is allocated
to the series so that the more recent records have the largest weight.
For example:

Series	730	860	1,360	1,750	1,580	1,650	1,970
Weights	1	2	3	4	5	6	7

and a weighted average is computed as:

$$\text{Average} = \frac{\sum(\text{Sales x appropriate weight})}{\sum \text{sum of weights}}$$

from above

$$= \frac{730 \times 1 + 860 \times 2 + 1,360 \times 3 \ldots \ldots \ldots 1,970 \times 7}{1 + 2 + 3 \ldots \ldots \ldots +7}$$

$$= \frac{45,120}{28} = 1,611$$

Such an average, whilst retaining some of the advantages of an average
based on a large number of data is more influenced by the values of
recent figures than by older records. Equally clear is that the
method is awkward to use with a general sequence of weights. A further
extension to this method is that of smoothing exponentially.

Exponential smoothing

Suppose that we already have an old forecast and new data has been received. It is almost certain that there will be a difference between the two figures. A forecast for the next period is required and we would wish to compensate for the previous differences. Because of the possibility of random fluctuations in the previous data, to allow the full difference may overcompensate and therefore some fraction of this difference would be more appropriate. We are therefore suggesting:

new forecast = old forecast + $\propto$ (latest observation - old forecast)

where $\propto$ is a fraction between 0 and 1. If we call the difference between the old forecast and latest observation the error, we have the new forecast being equivalent to the old forecast plus a fraction of this error. With the value of $\propto$ being a constant, calculation becomes easy when the latest observation is received and it does not require the keeping of extensive historical data.

By substituting in the equation values of 0 and 1 the stability and sensitivity of the forecast can be seen. When $\propto$ equals 0 the new forecast becomes the same as the old forecast irrespective of the latest observation. When $\propto$ equals 1 then the equation gives the new forecast as being equivalent to the latest observation. The former gives the ultimate in stability and the latter in sensitivity. What we require is a balance between the two and the value of $\propto$ determines this balance.

By continually forecasting using the equation quoted earlier, the new forecast is actually a weighted average of all the previous observations with the weights given to each observation not being the same, but decreasing by the fraction $(1 - \propto)$ as the observations before become more and more remote. The name 'exponential smoothing' thus derives from the fact that the observation decreases by this constant amount, $\propto$ being the 'smoothing constant'.

Selection of the smoothing constant

The larger the value selected as $\propto$ the more rapid will be the response to changes that actually occur. Usually a relatively high value, say $\propto$ = 0.5, is used for the first three months, so that the system automatically corrects the starting condition. High values could be used throughout where changes in demand pattern tend to persist for an appreciable period of time before any substantial change occurs.

The following table shows smoothing constants corresponding to given moving averages. Selection depends upon the nature of demand. If a small values were to be selected, e.g. $\propto$ = 0.01, response would be slow and gradual since this is equivalent to a moving average of 199 months. If a high value were selected, e.g. $\propto$ = 0.5 the response would be so rapid that random fluctuation would be reflected as well as a real change.

With $\propto$ being between 0.1 and 0.3 this represents a good compromise between a very stable system in which real changes pass undetected and a very nervous system that reflects every demand fluctuation.

Table 7.6.

Number of periods in equivalent moving average	Smoothing constant
3	0.500
4	0.400
5	0.333
6	0.286
7	0.250
8	0.222
9	0.200
12	0.154
18	0.105
19	0.100
24	0.080
36	0.054
39	0.050
48	0.041
199	0.010

Problems can occur, whereby a trend is detected several periods after its development and therefore there is a 'lag' in the system before this detection. Obviously we would like to pick up the trend and make the necessary correction. For this reason a second smoothing takes place in the form of:

new trend = $\propto$ (current trend) + (1 - $\propto$)(old trend)

The correction for the lag due to trend can then be expressed:

$$\text{expected demand} = \text{New Average} + \frac{(1 - \propto)}{\propto} \text{ (new trend)}$$

Table 7.7. shows an application of the three equations. The example shows calculations to forecast expected demand using a smoothing constant of 0.5 which is equivalent to a three month moving average. An explanation of the table and procedure is as follows:-

	Procedure
column (1) Date	Record date of current month.
column (2) Demand	Record demand during current month.
column (3) Average	Commence with an initial estimate. Here the average of the previous three months has been used. To get the average for the current month

column (3)(cont.)	multiply the previous average by $(1 \times \propto)$ and $\propto$ times the demand in the current month.
column (4) Change	From the average for the current month subtract the average calculated in the previous month.
column (5) Trend	Start with a trend equal to zero. Multiply this, and, thereafter, the trend which was calculated in the last month by $(1 - \propto)$ and add $\propto$ times the change for the current month.
column (6) Expected demand	Multiply the trend by $\dfrac{(1 - \propto)}{\propto}$ and add the average from column (3).

Conclusion

Great care must be taken in developing and applying any forecasting model. The value of experience and some intuition cannot be ignored, when combined with a satisfactory model. The further we try to forecast into the future the greater the number of variables required for consideration.

By comparing different forecasting methods using past data, useful information can be obtained in developing a satisfactory model.

Table 7.7.
Forecast in consumption

Date (1)	Demand (2)	New Average (3) Old Average x (1 - ∝) + Demand x ∝	Change in Average (4)
1977 Sept	11	19 x 0.5 = 9.5 + (11 x 0.5 = 5.5) = 15.0	-4.0
Oct	15	13.3 x 0.5 = 6.65 + (15 x 0.5 = 7.5) = 14.15	-0.85
Nov	18	13 x 0.5 = 6.5 + (18 x 0.5 = 9) = 15.5	+1.35
Dec	23	14.7 x 0.5 = 7.35 + (23 x 0.5 = 11.5) = 18.85	+3.35
1978 Jan	23	18.7 x 0.5 = 9.35 + (23 x 0.5 = 11.5) = 20.85	+2.0
Feb	24	21.3 x 0.5 = 10.65 + (24 x 0.5 = 12) = 22.65	+1.8
Mar	25	23.3 x 0.5 = 11.65 + (25 x 0.5 = 12.5) = 24.15	+1.5
Aprl	26	24 x 0.5 = 12 + (26 x 0.5 = 13) = 25	+0.85
May	43	25 x 0.5 = 12.5 + (43 x 0.5 = 21.5) = 33.8	+8.3
June	43	31.3 x 0.5 = 15.65 + (43 x 0.5 = 21.5) = 37.15	+3.35
July	24	37.3 x 0.5 = 18.15 + (24 x 0.5 = 12) = 30.15	-7.0
Aug	20	36.3 x 0.5 = 16.65 + (20.x 0.5 = 10) = 26.65	-3.5
Sept	16	29 x 0.5 = 14.5 + (16 x 0.5 = 8) = 22.5	-4.15
Oct	22	20 x 0.5 = 10 + (22 x 0.5 = 11) = 21	-1.5
Nov	27	19.7 x 0.5 = 9.85 + (27 x 0.5 = 13.5) = 23.35	+2.35
Dec	32	21.7 x 0.5 = 11.35 + (32 x 0.5 = 16) = 27.35	+4.0

Trend (5)	Forecast (6)
Last Trend x (1 -∝) + New Change in Average x ∝	New Trend x $\frac{(1 -∝)}{∝}$ + New Average
0 x ½ + -4.0 x ½ = -2.0	-2.0 x + 15.0 = 13.0
-2.0 x ½ + -0.85 x ½ = -1.42	-1.42 x 1 + 14.15 = 12.73
-1.42 x ½ + 1.35 x ½ = -0.03	-0.03 x 1 + 15.5 = 15.5
-0.03 x ½ + 3.35 x ½ = 1.64	1.64 x 1 + 18.85 = 20.49
1.64 x ½ + 2.0 x ½ = 1.82	1.82 x 1 + 20.85 = 22.67
1.82 x ½ + 1.8 x ½ = 1.81	1.81 x 1 + 22.65 = 24.46
1.81 x ½ + 1.5 x ½ = 1.65	1.65 x 1 + 24.15 = 25.80
1.65 x ½ + 0.85 x ½ = 1.25	1.25 x 1 + 25 = 26.25
1.25 x ½ + 8.3 x ½ = 4.75	4.75 x 1 + 33.8 = 38.55
4.75 x ½ + 3.35 x ½ = 4.05	4.05 x 1 + 37.15 = 41.20
4.05 x ½ + -7.0 x ½ = -1.48	-1.48 x 1 + 30.15 = 28.67
-1.48 x ½ + -3.5 x ½ = -2.49	-2.49 x 1 + 26.65 = 24.16
-2.49 x ½ + -4.15 x ½ = -3.32	-3.32 x 1 + 22.5 = 19.18
-3.32 x ½ + -1.5 x ½ = -2.41	-2.41 x 1 + 21 = 18.59
-2.41 x ½ + 2.35 x ½ = -0.03	-0.03 x 1 + 23.35 = 23.32
-0.03 x ½ + 4.0 x ½ = 1.97	1.97 x 1 + 27.35 = 29.32

EXERCISES

1. (a) Describe three methods of forecasting data.

   (b) Use one of the methods to forecast data for the completion of
       the given table:-

Observation	Forecast
12	10
14	
16	
18	
20	
22	

   (c) Comment on the degree of accuracy of the forecast results.

2. (a) The sales figures for a large industrial company for the
       period July 1977 to April 1978 have been rounded to the
       nearest £ million and are shown in the table below:

July 1977	83	December 1977	90
August 1977	90	January 1978	93
September 1977	101	February 1978	95
October 1977	99	March 1978	95
November 1977	94	April 1978	91

   By using a three monthly moving average calculate the trend
   in this data. Show the monthly figures and the trend figures
   graphically and estimate the sales for May 1978.

   (b) Using the figures for July 1977 to November 1977 calculate
       a three monthly exponentially weighted moving average using
       a factor of 0.5.

3. The unit cost 'y' of the production of a quantity 'x' of a product,
   with x being in thousands, is given by the following table:

x	1	3	4	8
y	9.9	9.7	9.6	9.2

   It has been assumed that 'x' and 'y' are related by an equation of
   the form, $y = mx + c$, where 'c' and 'm' are constants. Use the
   method of least squares to find 'c' and 'm'.

   Taking 'y' as the vertical axis and 'x' as the horizontal axis
   plot the given data and line of best fit.

SOLUTIONS TO EXERCISES

1. (a) Linear regression - method of least squares, which is suitable when two variables are present.

   Weighted averages - forecasting demand.

   Exponential smoothing - forecasting demand.

   (b) Choosing the exponential smoothing method, and using $\propto$ as 0.5 (say).

Observation	Forecast	Error	$\propto$ x Error	New Forecast
12	10	+2	1	11
14	11	+3	+1.5	12.5
16	12.5	+3.5	+1.8	14.3
18	14.3	+3.7	+1.9	16.2
20	16.2	+3.8	+1.9	18.1
22	18.1	+3.9	+2.0	20.1

   (c) The series has a linear trend with no random fluctuations, the forecast lags consistently behind the observation values. For the formula used:

   New average $= \propto$(new demand) $+ (1 - \propto)$(old average)

   this does not take account of the trend and therefore we would be required to smooth the trend values and incorporate this information in the new forecast.

2. (a)

Month	Year	Sales £ million	Three monthly total	Trend
July	1977	83		
August		90	274	91.3
September		101	290	96.7
October		99	294	98
November		94	283	94.3
December		90	277	92.3
January	1978	93	278	92.7
February		95	283	94.3
March		95	281	93.7
April		91		

189

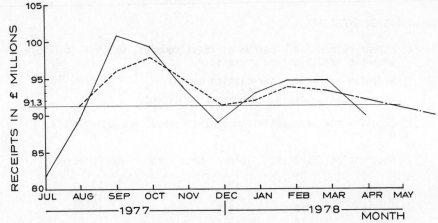

(b) Exponential weighted moving average is

$$\frac{A_3 + \propto A_2 + \propto^2 A_1}{1 + \propto + \propto^2}$$

A_3 = the most recent month, A_2 the preceding month, etc.

$\propto$ = the exponential factor.

(i) For July 1977 average:

$$= \frac{101 + 0.5 \times 90 + 0.25 \times 83}{1 + 0.5 + 0.25}$$

$$= \frac{101 + 45 + 20.75}{1.75}$$

$$= \frac{166.75}{1.75}$$

$$= 95.28.$$

(ii) For August 1977 average:

$$= \frac{99 + 0.5 \times 101 + 0.25 \times 90}{1.75}$$

$$= \frac{99 + 50.5 + 22.5}{1.75}$$

$$= \frac{172}{1.75} \qquad = \qquad 98.28$$

190

(iii) For September 1977 average:

$$= \frac{94 + 0.5 \times 99 + 0.25 \times 101}{1.75}$$

$$= \frac{94 + 49.5 + 25.25}{1.75}$$

$$= \frac{168.75}{1.75}$$

$$= 96.42$$

3.

x	y	xy	x^2
1	9.9	9.9	1
3	9.7	29.1	9
4	9.6	38.4	16
8	9.2	73.6	64
$\sum x = 16$	$\sum y = 38.4$	$\sum xy = 151$	$\sum x^2 = 90$

$$\sum y = Cn + m\sum x$$
$$\sum xy = C\sum x + m\sum x^2$$
$$38.4 = 4c + m16 \qquad\qquad (1)$$
$$151 = 16c + m90 \qquad\qquad (2)$$

multiply (1) through x 4

$$153.6 = 16c + m64$$
$$2.6 = -26m$$
$$\therefore m = -0.1$$

hence c = 10

equation of the line = y = -0.1x + 10.

191

Application

1. MIDSHIRE COTTON FABRICS

A small family concern manufacturing cotton dresses, shirts and blouses commence production in 1975. For a company entering such a competitive market the results had been very satisfactory, but without any experience in forecasting, insufficient stock levels had created many problems.

Fortunately data had been carefully kept by the company since commencing production on all three areas of production - shirts, dresses and blouses. The yearly turnover, however, is the only information available for the first two years, 1975 and 1976. For the years 1977 and 1978 the monthly turnover is available and all the data had been adjusted for holiday periods and sales days. The data available is presented in the following table:

Sales data for Midshire Cotton Fabrics

Year		Shirts £	Dresses £	Blouses £
1975		120,000	90,000	10,000
1976		110,000	100,000	20,000
1977	Jan	7,300	9,450	2,500
	Feb	7,700	8,100	2,325
	March	7,100	8,550	2,400
	April	8,800	9,550	2,475
	May	8,900	9,900	2,625
	June	9,700	8,900	2,750
	July	8,200	9,000	2,950
	August	6,600	8,550	2,800
	Sept	7,500	8,100	2,425
	Oct	7,900	8,050	2,250
	Nov	8,300	8,600	2,125
	Dec	7,600	11,250	2,375
	Total	96,000	108,000	30,000
1978	Jan	6,200	10,500	2,900
	Feb	6,550	9,050	2,850
	March	6,400	9,500	2,875
	April	7,700	10,450	3,075
	May	7,600	11,000	3,150
	June	8,300	10,150	4,300
	July	7,550	9,850	5,650
	August	5,750	9,500	6,350
	Sept	6,750	8,950	6,375
	Oct	7,100	9,050	7,725
	Nov	7,450	9,550	6,575
	Dec	6,650	12,450	9,850
	Total	84,000	120,000	61,675

It was decided to take the opportunity of employing a student undertaking his final year at university. A requirement of the course was that practical training and project work would be done in the final six months of the final academic year. The project was presented in four parts, as follows:

Project

Subject: Sale of shirts, dresses and blouses.

Problem: To forecast future sales for shirts, dresses and blouses.

Company requirements:

(1) To plot the data available in the three sales areas mentioned and indicate suggested trends for forecasting.

(2) Analyse the data for shirts and using the trend, seasonal factor and random variations, prepare a sales forecast for the years 1979 and 1980.

(3) Suggest a technique for forecasting the other two products, dresses and blouses.

(4) Exponential smoothing has been suggested as the method that should be used. Apply the method to the sales of blouses for the year 1978, using a constant of 0.2.

Discussion

In the form of a report comment on the results obtained. Explain how the forecasting methods could be improved using the data given.

193

Solution to application

1. MIDSHIRES COTTON FABRICS

Project Report

Subject: Sales of shirts, dresses and blouses.

Problem: To forecast future sales for shirts, dresses and blouses.

(1) The graphical presentation shows that for:
   (a) shirts, the linear trend is downwards;
   (b) dresses, the linear trend is upwards;
   (c) blouses, the linear trend is upwards, plus an exponential growth from the period June 1977.

(2) There are several methods that can be adopted to obtain the seasonal factor. The average seasonal factors are as follows:

January	90	July	105
February	95	August	83
March	90	September	95
April	111	October	100
May	110.5	November	104.5
June	120	December	95

It is suggested that the forecast for 1979 and 1980 be

1979 forecast - monthly sales = £6,000 x seasonal factor

1980 forecast - monthly sales = £5,000 x seasonal factor

(3) A reasonable technique for dresses is applying the linear upwards trend for 10% per annum.

For blouses, using the linear trend with superimposed growth, but lack of sufficient information for further estimation.

(4) Using exponential smoothing with $\propto = 0.2$

Results:

Period	Forecast	Actual	Error
December 1977	-	2,375	-
January 1978	2,375	2,900	+525
February	2,480	2,850	+270
March	2,534	2,875	+341
April	2,602	3,075	+473
May	2,697	3,150	+463
June	2,790	4,300	+510
July	2,892	5,650	+2,658
August	3,524	6,350	+2,826
September	4,087	6,375	+2,288
October	4,543	7,725	+3,180
November	5,179	6,575	+1,396
December	5,458	9,850	+4,392
January 1979	6,336		

Recommendations

Exponential smoothing in (4) is unsuitable when a rapid trend is present as it lags behind. Consider using double smoothing allowing for lag and compare results. In (2) confidence limits should be applied for a certain level of confidence and therefore figures presented can only be considered as a 'rough guide'. On reviewing these recommendations please state whether you wish them to be put into effect.

RANDOM SAMPLING NUMBERS

20 17	23 17	38 61	86 10	92 52	44 25
74 49	03 04	53 70	48 63	94 49	57 38
94 70	38 67	29 65	78 71	48 64	06 57
22 15	69 84	32 54	15 12	38 37	12 93
93 29	12 18	27 30	50 57	12 53	96 40
03 64	42 95	06 41	92 34	39 08	21 42
62 49	67 86	31 83	67 68	27 47	52 03
61 00	98 36	48 88	33 40	06 86	68 57
89 03	28 74	09 96	22 03	01 79	33 81
01 72	52 40	06 71	14 29	95 79	31 96
08 72	75 73	27 07	30 85	04 67	19 13
95 97	17 27	64 71	32 75	20 99	94 85
37 99	70 40	46 12	36 74	72 10	95 93
05 79	85 33	88 71	54 28	96 23	66 45
55 85	63 42	91 22	41 39	36 65	78 32
26 04	38 57	68 40	24 25	03 61	01 20
50 94	78 41	10 60	30 21	70 96	36 89
37 96	45 05	75 85	27 19	17 85	48 51
66 91	42 83	60 77	90 91	79 62	57 66
33 58	02 07	21 29	90 42	84 43	67 95
47 67	87 59	72 61	14 00	28 28	55 86
18 43	97 37	68 97	56 56	57 95	01 88
65 58	60 87	51 09	96 61	15 53	66 88
44 75	37 01	28 88	79 90	31 00	91 14
85 65	31 75	43 15	45 93	64 78	34 53
88 02	07 23	00 15	59 05	16 09	94 42
77 97	99 45	69 85	51 87	85 56	45 04
44 91	99 49	94 60	06 77	59 25	08 51
91 02	19 96	47 59	89 65	27 84	30 92
63 37	26 24	23 66	04 50	65 04	65 56
82 42	70 51	55 04	61 47	88 83	99 34
73 49	82 37	32 70	17 72	03 61	66 26
60 53	91 17	33 26	44 70	93 14	99 70
49 05	74 48	10 55	35 25	24 28	20 22
35 66	66 34	25 35	91 23	49 74	37 25
97 26	42 23	01 28	59 58	92 69	03 66
73 82	20 26	22 43	88 08	19 85	08 12
47 65	56 07	97 85	56 79	48 87	77 96

DISCOUNT FACTORS

Present value of £1 receivable at the end of each period:

Year			Percentage			
	5	8	10	12	14	15
1	.952	.926	.909	.893	.877	.870
2	.907	.857	.826	.797	.769	.756
3	.864	.794	.751	.712	.675	.658
4	.823	.735	.683	.636	.592	.572
5	.784	.681	.621	.567	.519	.497
6	.746	.630	.564	.507	.456	.432
7	.711	.583	.513	.452	.400	.376
8	.677	.540	.467	.404	.351	.327
9	.645	.500	.424	.361	.308	.284
10	.614	.463	.386	.322	.270	.247
11	.585	.429	.350	.287	.237	.215
12	.557	.397	.319	.257	.208	.187
13	.530	.368	.290	.229	.182	.163
14	.505	.340	.263	.205	.160	.141
15	.481	.315	.239	.183	.140	.123
16	.458	.292	.218	.163	.123	.107
17	.436	.270	.198	.146	.108	.093
18	.416	.250	.180	.130	.095	.081
19	.396	.232	.164	.116	.083	.070
20	.377	.215	.149	.104	.073	.061
21	.359	.199	.135	.093	.064	.053
22	.342	.184	.123	.083	.056	
23	.326	.170	.112	.074		
24	.310	.158	.102	.066		
25	.295	.146	.092	.059		
30	.231	.099	.057			
35	.181	.068	.036			
40	.142	.046	.022			

Bibliography

1. Bross, I.D., Design for Decisions, Macmillan, New York 1953.
2. Bursk, Edward C., and Chapman, John F. (Eds), New Decision Making Tools for Managers, Harvard University Press, Cambridge, Massachusetts.
3. Chernoff, H., and Moses, L.E., Elementary Decision Theory, Wiley, New York 1959.
4. Churchman, C. West, Prediction and Optimal Decision , Prentice Hall, New York 1962.
5. Dalton, M., Men who Manage, Wiley, New York 1959.
6. Davidson, D. et al., Decision Making, Stanford University Press, California 1957.
7. Forrester, J., Industrial Dynamics, Wiley, New York 1961.
8. Johnson, Rossall J., Executive Decisions, South Western Publishing Company, Cincinnati 1963.
9. Jones, M.H., Executive Decision Making, Irwin, Illinois 1957.
10. Koontz, H. and O'Donnell, C.J., Principles of Management, McGraw-Hill, New York 1959.
11. Lindsay, F.A., New Techniques for Management Decision Making, McGraw-Hill, New York 1963.
12. Simon, H.A., The New Science of Management Decision, Harper and Row, New York, 1960.
13. Taylor, F.W., Scientific Management, Harper and Brothers, New York 1947.
14. Thrall, R.M., Decision Processes, Wiley, New York 1954.

NETWORK PLANNING

15. Battersby, A., Network Analysis for Planning and Scheduling, Macmillan, London 1970.
16. Brennan, J., Application of Critical Path Techniques, English Universities Press, London 1968.
17. McLaren, K.G. and Buesnel, E.L., Network Analysis in Project Management, Cassell, London 1969.
18. Scutt, C. W., Critical Path Method: Users Guide, Fisons Fertilisers Ltd., Felixstowe, 1965.
19. Thornley, G. (Ed), Critical Path Analysis in Practice, Tavistock Press, 1968.

REPLACEMENT

20. Alchian, A.A., Economic Replacement Policy, Rand Corporation Report R-224 April 1952, and RM-2153, April 1958.
21. Barlow, R.E., and Prochan, F., Mathematical Theory of Reliability, Wiley, New York 1965.
22. Bazovsky, J., Reliability: Theory and Practice, Prentice-Hall, Englewood Cliffs, N.J. 1961.
23. Cox, D.R., Renewal Theory, Methuen, London 1962.

24. Dean, J., Capital Budgeting, Columbia University Press, New York 1951.
25. Lloyd, D.K. and Lepow, M., Reliability, Management Methods and Mathematics, Prentice Hall, Englewood Cliffs, N.J. 1962.
26. Roberts, N.H., Mathematical Methods in Reliability Engineering, McGraw-Hill, New York, 1964.
27. Terborgh, B., Dynamic Equipment Policy, McGraw-Hill, New York 1949.

SIMULATION

28. Forrester, J.W., Industrial Dynamics, Wiley, 1961.
29. Malcolm, D.G., Bibliography on the Use of Simulation in Management Analysis, Operations Research, 8, 169-177, 1960.
30. Meyer, M.A. (Ed), Symposium on Monte Carlo Methods, Wiley, New York 1956.
31. Morgenthaler, G.E., The Theory and Application of Simulation in Operations Research, in Progress in Operations Research, Vol.1, Ackoff, R. L. (Ed).
32. Rivett, P., Trends in Operational Research, from The Product Engineer, 44, p.109, 1965.
33. Tocher, K.D., The Art of Simulation, English Universities Press, 1963.

FORECASTING

34. Anon., An Introduction to Business Forecasting, Institute of Cost and Works Accountants, London 1960.
35. Brown, R.G. Statistical Forecasting for Inventory Control, McGraw-Hill, New York, 1959.
36. Berners-Lee, C.M., Models for Decision, English University Press, London 1965.
37. Coutie, G.A., Davies, O.L., Hossell, C.H., Millar, D.W., G.P., and Morrell, A.J.H., Short Term Forecasting, Oliver and Boyd, Edinburgh 1964.
38. Freund, J.E. and Williams, F.J., Modern Business Statistics, Pitman, London 1959.
39. Gregg, J.V., Hossell, C.H. and Richardson, J.T., Mathematical Trend Curves: An Aid to Forecasting, Oliver and Boyd, Edinburgh 1964.
40. Shaw, L.W., Management Information and Statistical Method, The General Educational Trust of the Institute of Chartered Accountants in England and Wales, London 1968.
41. Spiegel, M.R., Theory and Problems of Statistics, Schaum Publishing Co., New York 1961.

LINEAR PROGRAMMING

42. Charnes, Abraham and Cooper, W.W., Management Models and Industrial Applications of Linear Programming, Wiley, New York 1961.
43. Cooper, W.W. and Henderson, A., Introduction to Linear Programming, Wiley, New York 1953.
44. Dantzig, G.B., Linear Programming and Extensions, Princeton University Press, Princeton 1963.
45. Hadley, G., Linear Algebra, Addison-Wesley, Reading Mass. 1961.

46. Levin, R.I. and Lamone, R.P., Linear Programming for Management Decisions, Irwin, Homewood, Illinois 1969.
47. Meisels, K., A Primer to Linear Programming, New York University Press, New York 1962.
48. Metzger, R.W., Elementary Mathematical Programming, Wiley, New York 1958.
49. Sasieni, M., Yaspan, A., and Friedman, L., Operations Research - Methods and Problems, Wiley, New York 1959.

Index